WHEN SATAN
WORE A CROSS

By Fred Rosen

WHEN SATAN WORE A CROSS
THERE BUT FOR THE GRACE OF GOD

WHEN SATAN WORE A CROSS

FRED ROSEN

HARPER

An Imprint of HarperCollins*Publishers*

HARPER

An Imprint of HarperCollins*Publishers*
10 East 53rd Street
New York, New York 10022-5299

Copyright © 2007 by Fred Rosen
ISBN: 978-0-7394-9099-0

Printed in the United States of America

For Greg Rose for his support,
Allison Hock for her inspiration,
and both for their friendship.

CONTENTS

. . . sooner or later, somewhere, somehow, we must settle with the world and make payment for what we have taken.

FRAN STRIKER

From the cowardice that shrinks from new truth, From the laziness that is content with half truths, From the arrogance that thinks it knows all truth, O God of truth, deliver us.

HUGH B. BROWN

AUTHOR'S NOTE

This book is based upon on-the-spot reporting and interviewing in Toledo, Ohio, follow-up interviews, official court and police documents, and other background research materials, including published news accounts.

Dialogue has been reconstructed on the basis of the participants' recollections, as well as the official record of the case. In a few instances, the names of people, and some background information in their lives, were changed to protect anonymity. Where public documents have been reprinted, personal and identifiable information have been deleted.

Prologue

June 4, 2006

They threw my bag off the train about dawn.

It was the headline a month earlier that had gotten to me: "Priest Kills Nun." If it was true, it was a first in American criminal history.

Reverend Father Gerald Robinson, sixty-eight years old, had been accused of murdering seventy-one-year-old nun Sister Margaret Ann Pahl twenty-six years earlier in 1980. It was a cold case, the cable channels trumpeted, solved by modern forensic science. The prosecution had approached trial with great confidence, the defense with great diffidence.

Every day, national TV covered the day's events in the courtroom. The prosecution alleged that Father Robinson murdered Sister Pahl because there was "bad blood" between them. Pushed to the breaking point, he strangled and stabbed her more than thirty times. That's a lot of anger. The trial included testimony from an exorcist—yes, an exorcist—who told the jury that the killer carved an inverted crucifix into Sister Pahl's chest.

The inverted cross is a satanic symbol used in the Black Mass of the Middle Ages. A parody of the Catholic Mass in which the supplicant worships Satan or one of his demons, the Black Mass is celebrated *backwards*, with the last ritual practiced first and so forth. The ritual of how to blaspheme the cross is left up to the supplicant. One way is to spit on it, another to invert it. Even after conviction, it wasn't clear if Father Robinson was indeed a Satanist who had practiced the Black Mass.

None it of it made any sense.

I had boarded in Albany the afternoon before and settled into my seat for the eleven-hour ride on the Lake Shore Limited to Toledo. Outside the window, the forests of the upper Catskills rushed by, seeming to bloom dark green before my eyes. Late afternoon sunshine waned into the blue light of dusk. The train passed over a river that became a black sea stretching into impenetrable darkness. Passengers dozed into the night, awakened only by the conductor announcing upcoming stations.

Toledo is in the upper northwest corner of Ohio. Its access to the Maumee River, which connects to the commercially vital Lake Erie, made the city a major economic prize to the state that possessed it. In the nineteenth century, Michigan and Ohio put in bids for ownership; Ohio won.

"Toledo, next!" the conductor's harsh voice cut into the early morning darkness.

The train passed a crossing. A moment later, the engineer applied the brake and the train glided on silent rails into the Amtrak station. Jumping down, I grabbed my bag and picked my way gently across two sets of tracks set in gravel before reaching the station platform and, beyond it, the empty waiting room. There were no cabs at the curb, but the station agent, behind a long faux marble plastic counter lit from above by unearthly fluorescents, readily volunteered to call one.

"Alex can use the fare," she said, referring to the local cabdriver on duty.

"That's awfully nice of you to call. They wouldn't do that in New York."

She laughed.

"You're in the Midwest."

Alex pulled his cab up a ramp and into a gray twilight that brightened over a strange urban landscape. On the shores of the Maumee River were the colorful, architecturally futuristic headquarters of the Dow Corning company. On the other side of this huge boulevard was some sort of combination of old brick buildings saved from the wrecker's ball because someone had rented them, and empty lots.

The cabbie turned into Erie Boulevard. Despite extensive renovations meant to make them attractive to merchants, most of the storefronts were vacant. I wondered if Ohio might want to sell the place back to Michigan.

"The murder trial of the priest got things going a little," said the clerk behind the counter of the Radisson. "The cable TV people were here a long time and everyone else. Now it's quieted down ever since the verdict."

What the clerk didn't know was that since the trial, a

new accuser had come forward. Identified in court documents as "Jane Doe," she claimed that Robinson raped, sodomized, and did all kinds of unspeakable acts to her during satanic ceremonies for a number of years when she was a child. Jane Doe's case was coming before the court tomorrow.

It was a Sunday, which just made the downtown deader than usual. There was no diner to go to for coffee, no place for a sandwich, nothing within a half-mile trek across hostile territory. Toledo's homicide rate is one murder per 10,042 people, more than 30 percent higher than New York City's. From my tenth-floor room, I looked out as the daylight quickly overtook the decrepit buildings, giving it all a slight glow, like there was something there worth killing over.

I pulled heavy drapes, blocked out the new day, and got into bed, wondering how Sister Margaret Ann Pahl had come to be the unluckiest of the Toledo 10,042.

PART ONE

CHAPTER 1

Somebody's Daughter

1909

Long before the medical examiner's knife enters her thorax, a female murder victim starts out as somebody's daughter.

President Taft had just installed his jumbo girth in the White House. Back in his home state of Ohio, the rural hamlet of Edgerton had not yet been completely wired for electricity. It was in Edgerton that Margaret Ann Pahl came into the world on April 6, 1909. Margaret Ann was the fourth of nine children born to farmers Frank and Catherine Pahl.

Devout Catholics, the Pahls followed all the precepts of the Catholic Church and believed faithfully in the seven sacraments within which Christ dwells: baptism, confession, the Eucharist, confirmation, marriage, holy orders (ordination to the ministry), and extreme unction (anointing the sick, dying, and dead). The Pahls believed in passing on these beliefs and values to their children.

As Margaret Ann grew older, she attended Catholic school, where she learned that of the seven sacraments, the most important was the Eucharist. At first glance, the Eucharist is simply a wafer and some wine. But during the third part of the Catholic Mass, the Liturgy of the Eucharist, *transubstantiation* takes place. When the priest says the Eucharistic Prayer over the wafer and wine, they transubstantiate, or change literally into the body and blood of Christ, which are then ingested by the parishioners who come forward to take Communion.

During her growing-up years, Margaret Ann took Communion many times. She discovered that after Mass, the consecrated hosts were placed for 363 days in the tabernacle. The tabernacle is a fixed lock box usually placed on the main altar of the church. It was there almost all year for parishioners to venerate. Only on Good Friday, the day Christ was crucified, and on Holy Saturday, the day before his Resurrection, was the Eucharist stored in the sacristy, the dressing room adjacent to the church chapel. Such detail fascinated Margaret Ann and made her feel part of something greater than herself.

Margaret Ann finished high school shortly after her eighteenth birthday in 1927. While America blithely danced the Charleston away into the Great Depression, and Calvin Coolidge made less money than Babe Ruth precisely because of that, Margaret Ann had decided to serve her Lord. It is hard to say exactly when, but by the time she finished high school, it was clear to family and friends alike that she had been touched by God's vision for her life.

Margaret Ann would serve him by becoming a novitiate in the Sisters of Mercy, the order founded by Catherine McAuley in Dublin, Ireland, a century earlier. Margaret Ann had been divinely inspired by no less a person than the nineteenth century's Mother Teresa.

Such is Catherine McAuley's continued popularity that her image graces the most recent Irish five-pound note. The painting on the bill shows a woman with piercing black eyes, a long aquiline nose, thin lips, and a strong, resolute chin. Catherine is wearing the traditional Sisters of Mercy black and white headdress that would become their trademark.

There was gentleness to Catherine, but behind that piercing gaze was a clear, steely resolve she inherited from her father. Catherine was born September 29, 1787, at Stormanstown House, a private estate in Dublin, Ireland. The first of three children born to James McAuley, Catherine realized early that her father came from an old and distinguished Irish Catholic family that had managed to survive when Catholicism had been all but crushed in Ireland. James McAuley spent more than he could afford to help the poor and infirm. The example was not lost on the young Catherine.

After McAuley died in 1794, his widow couldn't get her financial affairs in order. Forced to sell Stormanstown House, she moved with her brood to Dublin. There, the *Catholic Encyclopedia* says, "the family came so completely under the influence of Protestant fashionable society that all, with the exception of Catherine, became Protestants. She revered the memory of her father too greatly to embrace a religion he abhorred."

Tragedy struck the McAuley family yet again when the Widow McAuley suddenly died. The three orphaned McAuley children were passed along to a distant family member who squandered their inheritance. As they were passed along again and again like so much human detritus, each "guardian" did the best he could to drum the Protestant Reformation into their heads.

At first, Catherine flat-out refused—a perilous position for a female orphan without tuppence to her name. A single woman without money or prospects in early nineteenth-century Dublin had no rights. Some of Catherine's good friends emphatically tried to convince her to support an arranged marriage. Catherine, of course, declined. She was dogged in refusing to be told how to think, let alone what to do.

Finally, in the interests of family peace, she agreed to experience Protestantism before totally condemning it. Her researches only served to reinforce her Catholic beliefs. She didn't like the Protestant "dissensions and contradictions, the coldness and the barrenness of its spiritual life." It is at this point that Catherine McAuley should have disappeared into the pages of history. But she didn't.

A wealthy relative of Catherine's mother, Simon T. Callahan, suddenly returned from India in 1803. He bought Coolock House a few kilometers outside Dublin, and adopted Catherine. She came to live with her second father on his estate. Soon Catherine showed that she had not forgotten the lessons of James McAuley's charity.

For the next two decades, Catherine spent some of Callahan's fortune in the service of the Catholic sick and poor. The compromise was that Callahan, a Protestant, would not allow any Church icons into his home. It was a fair bargain, but Catherine worked on him. On his deathbed in 1822, Callahan's hard Protestant heart finally melted. Baptized a Catholic, Callahan took his first Communion and then died, leaving his entire fortune to Catherine.

The sudden turn in her circumstances was not lost on Catherine.

Suddenly presented with the financial means to make a difference, she used the rest of Callahan's money to finance her vision of extreme unction. It took five years, but in 1827, Catherine and two female friends founded a new institution for destitute women and orphans, as well as a school for the poor. While the institution was not directly affiliated with the Church, it was decidedly Catholic in its approach and took its marching orders from the archbishop.

Catherine decided that she and her friends would wear a nunlike uniform—simple black dress and cape flowing to the belt, white collar, lace cap, and veil. Watching the congregation that Catherine had put together, the archbishop could see that the day was coming when it would be part of the Church. How could it not be? The archbishop asked Catherine for a name by which her group could be called.

Given her vision and its success, Catherine must have known that this moment would come. She had evidently thought hard on the matter because she quickly replied, "The Sisters of Mercy." Catherine decided to adopt the roll-up-the-sleeve-and-get-something-done practicality of the Sisters of Charity with the existential dedication and silent prayers of the Carmelites. She knew that her mission now was to undertake works of mercy for the rest of her life.

The Church, however, felt threatened by Catherine's continued independence. She looked and acted like a Catholic nun without being one. More importantly, neither Catherine nor her institution was under the archdiocese's direct control. The archbishop decided that it was time for Catherine to declare her intentions—was hers a Catholic institution or not? The pressure was put on.

Catherine held a meeting with her associates, who now numbered twelve. They voted unanimously to become a Catholic religious congregation. Hewing closely to Catherine's independent streak, the Sisters of Mercy would be unaffiliated with any existing community of nuns. But now the Sisters of Mercy's would be part of the Church.

Like other Catholic nunneries, the Sisters of Mercy would lead an ordered and regimented life of prayer, choir, chastity, and poverty. Catherine decided, however, that the Sisters of Mercy would specifically tend to the poor, the destitute, the infirm, and also provide education for those who could not afford it, at a time when most couldn't.

In 1829, two years after the Sisters of Mercy had opened their doors, the archbishop said a prayer and blessed the chapel, dedicating it to Our Lady of Mercy. Being a nun, though, was a lot more than just saying you were one. You had to become a novitiate at a nunnery and receive the proper religious training. Catherine decided she and two other Sisters of Mercy, Elizabeth Harley and Anna Maria Doyle, would begin their novitiate at George's Hill, Dublin, on September 8, 1830.

A little more than one year later on December, 12, 1831, they took their formal vows. Thus did Catherine McAuley become Sister Mary Catherine. Appointed first superior of the Sisters of Mercy, she held the post for the rest of her life, until her death at age fifty-four in 1841. By then, the Sisters of Mercy had spread out across the British Isles, into the Commonwealth, including Australia, New Zealand, Scotland, and Canada. At every stop, they became known for their tender kindnesses and good works.

Bishop Michael O'Connor of Pittsburgh, Pennsylvania, saw how effective the sisters were at helping the poor and sick. He asked for and received help from the Sisters of Mercy. A group of sisters was dispatched from Ireland to Pittsburgh. On December 22, 1843, the Sisters of Mercy opened their first congregation in the United States. By 1847, they took over the management of the first hospital in western Pennsylvania. Eighty years later in 1927, Catherine McAuley's vision inspired eighteen-year-old Margaret Ann Pahl to get into the backseat of her parents' Buick touring car to serve God.

Since Edgerton was in the far western part of the state directly abutting Indiana, the trip was a good seventy-five miles east on rutted dirt roads, passing Bowling Green until taking a direct dogleg south. Then it was another thirty miles of spine-jarring "roadway" before getting to the outskirts of Tiffin, Ohio. It was here in the early 1920s that the Sisters of Mercy opened their Ohio novitiate, Our Lady of the Pines. It was Margaret Ann's final destination.

After dropping Margaret Ann off and seeing her settled into the nunnery, her family turned around and trudged back home. After another bone-jarring hundred-mile trip, they arrived back in Edgerton to find that Margaret Ann had left behind all her material belongings. Patiently and neatly, she had attached notes to everything indicating which sibling got what.

For her part, Margaret Ann never looked back.

As America careened through the twentieth century, the Sisters of Mercy were not far behind, picking up the human detritus that "progress" cast aside. They established a hospital system that they administered across the United States. Trained as a registered nurse, Margaret Ann stayed in Ohio, working within what would become known as the Mercy Healthcare system.

Showing a talent for administration, she became the director of the Sisters of Mercy's nursing school. Further along in her career, she became administrator at St. Charles Hospital in Oregon, Ohio, right across the Maumee River from Toledo, and Mercy Hospital back in Tiffin. In between, Margaret Ann had a lively social life, visiting nuns throughout the northeast and family back in Edgerton, and taking trips throughout the northeast. She particularly loved Niagara Falls. Margaret Ann loved listening to opera. It was a passion.

During her long career, Margaret Ann, a trained nurse, would have noted that alcoholism was a problem for some priests, and that those who couldn't control their drinking wound up reconciled to backwater parishes and assignments. In Toledo, Mercy Hospital was one of those backwater parishes. Of the two hospital priests, Jerome Swiatecki was a known alcoholic. Staffers talked of Gerald Robinson being more of a private drinker. As for the venue, Catherine McCauley's spiritual heirs had their work cut out for them.

Mercy Hospital was located in a high-crime area, serving a predominantly low-income African-American population. On Friday and Saturday nights you had to take a ticket to get into the emergency room. Gunshot and knife wounds came first. The place served a desperate, disenfranchised community. In the middle of it all were the Sisters of Mercy who administered the hospital.

The one place to get away from this emotionally charged atmosphere was the hospital chapel, a small affair, set up in traditional Catholic style. Four rows, of two wooden chairs each, faced the altar up front, the tabernacle to the side and behind, and on the right, the sacristy. The chapel had two entrances, one behind the altar and one inside the room itself. The one in the room, Margaret Ann soon discovered, took you through a clean, sterile white corridor that led to a stairwell. The stairwell connected to the dormitory area, where many of the people who worked in the hospital, including the Sisters of Mercy, lived.

In the nuns' dormitory, there were no private showers or bathrooms. Everything was shared by the sisters. None of the rooms had TVs or phones, except that of Sister Phyllis Ann, the hospital director. It was here, at Mercy Hospital, that Margaret Ann found herself assigned in the twilight of her career.

As she approached her seventy-first birthday in April 1980, Margaret Ann's hearing had faded. Now partially deaf, she was too proud to wear a hearing aid, and was considering retirement. Her assignments had been reduced to making certain the chapel was in readiness for the priests when they gave their services and making certain the nuns' dormitory rooms were cleaned.

Shirley Ann Lucas, forty-four years old, was the Mercy Hospital housekeeper, whose job it was to clean the rooms. Sister Margaret would leave open the doors to the rooms to be cleaned. By prior agreement, if any room had the door closed, Lucas would not enter. The only personal rooms she cleaned were those of any guests who occupied the convent and Sister Phyllis Ann's room.

On Good Friday, April 4, 1980, Lucas was cleaning a guest's room, when Sister Margaret walked by. They stopped to chat. Lucas had always found Sister Margaret to be a fussy individual who liked things her own way, a very strict and devoted Catholic.

That day she was especially upset.

"One of the priests wants to change the Good Friday service, and make it shorter," Sister Margaret Ann shouted in horror, breaking down and crying bitter tears.

"Why did they cheat God out of what was *his*?"

To a devoted Catholic like Sister Margaret, any change from established orthodoxy was heretical. The Church was her whole life. To see even a portion of it altered by someone, let alone a priest, was blasphemy!

The priest she was referring to was Gerald Robinson. Only he could make the changes to the Mass because he was the head priest. Margaret Ann's feelings toward Gerald Robinson were as close as she ever came in her life to hating someone.

For sixteen years since his ordination in 1964, Jerry

Robinson had been a popular priest in Toledo, a blue-collar city of about three hundred thousand, where a quarter of the citizens are Catholics. The Polish community especially liked Robinson, who sometimes spoke Polish during sermons and heard confessions in Polish. He had been educated at a seminary in Michigan that trained priests especially to minister to the Polish Catholic community that dominate many of the northern cities of Ohio and southern ones of Michigan.

Jerry Robinson was a local Toledo kid who had to make good. Ordained in 1964 at age twenty-six, he was a strikingly handsome man with a receding hairline of wavy, dark blond hair, dark piercing eyes, a straight nose, and a determined mouth and chin. Unfortunately for Robinson, it was 1964, not 1864.

Toledo's Polish-speaking Roman Catholics were in a decline that mirrored the society that had changed dramatically around them. Keeping the old ways alive was a fine idea, but in practice assimilation takes over. Pretty soon even the newest immigrants are anxious to speak English. That was Robinson's first problem—a shrinking clientele.

The second was that just like everywhere else in the country, Toledo was seeing its white urban population shrinking. Once again there was the modern version of the Oklahoma Land Rush, "white flight" to the suburbs. Even social circumstances were conspiring against him.

By 1980, Jerry Robinson was forty-two but looked fifty-two. His face had a puffy look it didn't have before, probably from his regular drinking. Jerry Robinson's once wavy, dark blond hair was now a crescent of gray. His eyes seemed hooded and sad. His mouth was creased into a slight, sarcastic smile. As the Polish Catholics disappeared through whatever social process was at work throughout the 1970s, Robinson had been transferred from one church to another. Never did he rise to head priest at any parish, until finally he found his way to the backwater duties as the head chaplain at Mercy Hospital.

On Good Friday, 1980, the television in the nun's communal room was turned on.

At 8 P.M., the choice was Bill Bixby's brilliant take on Dr. Jekyll in CBS's *The Incredible Hulk,* with Arnold Schwarzenegger's favorite doormat, Lou Ferrigno, as the big green guy. Or ABC's *Fantasy Island* with Ricardo Montalban and Herve ("Da plane, boss, da plane") Villechaize.

Nine P.M. was even better. There was the *Dukes of Hazzard* with a blond guy, a brunette guy, a brunette girl in shorts, and a car that was the star of it all, the General Lee. The real gem was on NBC. The nuns' favorite (and everyone else's) was James Garner in *The Rockford Files*. To a nun from Toledo used to poverty and dreariness in her surroundings, having a trailer on Malibu Beach and solving murders with charm and guile in the pursuit of justice, like Rockford, was extremely appealing.

No one afterward recalled the time Margaret Ann went to bed. No one could say for certain what was on her mind except for one thing: just as she had been taught back in Edgerton, she had responsibilities in the morning that she needed to fulfill. She was an "old school" nun and everyone knew it.

* * *

Routine is something that a smart murderer relies on. If he knows where his victim is going to be and when, working backwards it becomes easy to plan the crime. The essential point is to have enough time to do what is necessary, to kill at the right moment, literally when no one's looking, especially the victim. It also helps if you plan out how you are going to do it. Will you use your hands, for example, or rely on a weapon?

A gun perhaps? Guns were pretty messy. It was easy in that part of Toledo to obtain one on the street. But that cost money. Besides, he was not a professional; he had no idea where to go to get a Saturday night special. Anyway, a gun was too loud and would attract attention. He decided he wouldn't need one.

No, something easy to stab with.

That was how he finally decided he was going to do it.

But so what if he killed her? It wasn't enough. He wanted *to get her.* He made up his mind to do something *special,* just for her, for Sister Margaret Ann whom everyone knew and loved. Something special, to celebrate her union with Christ.

CHAPTER 2

Holy Saturday

April 5, 1980

Holy Saturday is the only day in the Catholic calendar when there is no morning Mass.

In Toledo, Margaret Ann awakened that morning in her seventh-floor Mercy Hospital dormitory room to the sharp ring of her electric alarm clock. Reaching out with a small, wrinkled hand, she pushed in the off button. Settling back, she did not get up until the second clock, a wind-up, went off at 5:30.

Even one day shy of her seventy-first birthday, Margaret Ann was as meticulous as the young girl who had labeled her belongings and left them behind for her siblings in Edgerton so long ago. But the years had taken their toll. Margaret Ann's hearing was failing, causing particular friction with Father Robinson, who resented having to continually repeat his instructions to her. She also could be forgetful, especially if she had something else on her mind. It was Robinson, as the hospital's chief chaplain, who had decided—and God only knew for his own reasons—to shorten yesterday's Good Friday service, causing Margaret Ann to cry.

Outside, it was a cloudy day. Audrey Garraway arrived for work at the usual time, about 6 A.M. She entered through a side door that had to be opened from the inside; she didn't have a key. Sister Margaret was always there to open it. Today for some reason she wasn't there. Surprised, Audrey went to the kitchen to get a key that would allow her to enter the dining area to start her workday.

At about the same time, Margaret Ann, now dressed in the traditional Sisters of Mercy habit, took the elevator down from the seventh floor. Turning left on the ground floor, she said, hello to Sue Bentley at the switchboard, continuing on to the hospital cafeteria. At about 6:15 A.M., Audrey ran into Sister Margaret in the sisters' dining area. She was carrying a green cafeteria tray.

"How'd you get into the kitchen?" Margaret Ann asked, remembering the duty she had forgotten to do that morning.

"I got the key from dietary," Audrey answered.

A few seconds later, Audrey saw Sister Margaret go out into the hallway. Drifting out of Audrey's view, Margaret Ann stopped at a supply closet. Using a key, she opened the padlock and took out cleaning cloths and incense. She placed them on the green tray, locked the closet again, and set off down the twisting halls of the hospital.

When she arrived a minute later at the twin wooden doors of the hospital chapel, they too were locked. That was expected at such an early hour. It was her job to prepare the chapel for the morning service. Even though there was none this morning, Margaret Ann remained a creature of habit. Opening the doors with the set of keys she carried, she switched on the chapel lights.

At about 6:20 A.M., Audrey saw Margaret Ann come back into the cafeteria. She was still carrying an empty cafeteria tray that she quickly filled up with raisin bran, grapefruit, and coffee. Margaret Ann ate the repast alone, seemingly lost in thought, which Audrey interrupted.

"Sister Margaret," she said brightly.

Margaret Ann looked up from her thoughts.

"Could you please tell me, Sister, when services are going to be scheduled for Holy Saturday?"

"They will be at seven o'clock," she answered. "Tonight."

Outside the hospital, Glenn Thomas expertly tooled his ambulance up around the hospital's circling driveway and parked. He had just finished his ambulance run to nearby St. Vincent Hospital. Hungry, he decided to go over to Mercy to get something to eat. Parking close to the entrance, he walked into the building just as the sun was coming up.

Glenn looked at his watch. It was 6:30 A.M. Inside, he headed straight for the cafeteria. Walking through the swinging doors, he ran into Sister Margaret. She was leaving and carrying an empty green cafeteria tray.

"Good morning, Sister Margaret," he said respectfully.

Glenn knew Margaret Ann as the sister who took an interest in his work and always talked to him when he had problems with his ambulance runs. This morning, she hustled past him and out the exit door, barely acknowledging his presence.

Once out of Glenn's view, Margaret Ann walked straight back to the chapel. At about 6:48 A.M., she opened the chapel doors. The pews were still empty. With no service scheduled until the evening, the only people in today would be the occasional sister saying her daily prayers, and perhaps relatives of patients. They would get to know the terrazzo floor intimately.

It was fitting that the chapel had a terrazzo floor. As a flooring material, it's two thousand years old. It became popular just about the time Jesus Christ walked the earth. Since then, it has become known as a mosaic type of flooring, made by the unique combination of embedding tiny pieces of marble in mortar and then polishing them. The mixture consists of two parts marble to one of cement. During the installation process additional marble chips are sprinkled on the surface so that at least 70 percent of the exposed surface is marble.

Terrazzo flooring is particularly good for high-traffic areas, like a chapel or sacristy. The marble, unlike the cement in the mixture, is almost nonabsorbent. Most things that stain just about anything else will not stain terrazzo.

Margaret Ann went up to the altar. She began polishing it with the cleaning cloths she had dropped off earlier. At some point, she needed to go into the sacristy to get the hosts for the evening's service. Holy Saturday is one of only two days on the Catholic calendar when the Holy Eucharist is stored in the sacristy.

The door into the sacristy was to the right of the altar. The sacristy in the hospital chapel was especially small. Only five hundred hosts were stored in the room. Margaret Ann took out her keys again and inserted one in the lock of the door, placed at the right of the altar.

Inside, the killer listened as the tumblers clicked into place. He had planned well. Holy Saturday was the only morning of the year when he would have a guarantee that no one would be there early in the hospital chapel. Plenty of time to do his work.

Margaret Ann pushed the door open. It was dark inside. Her small, frail figure was momentarily silhouetted by the chapel lights behind her. Killing her didn't exactly require a .44 Magnum. But planned murders require restraint. Pounce too early, and it attracts attention. Do it too late, and there was always the chance the victim could get away. It had to be timed well to work.

He chose to remain quietly in the shadows, until the door was closed behind her. Once she was safely in the room, the killer began the death work with his hands. He had confidence they could do the job, especially considering he got her neck from behind. If he strangled her from the front, it gave her a chance to defend herself by striking out at him. The last thing he needed were scratches on his face to identify him as the killer. He also had the weapon in his clothes to be used at the right time.

Strangling is a particularly personal way of killing a human being. As an additional benefit, nothing would be left behind, like fibers, if he had worn gloves. On the negative side, if his nails dug into her skin, there'd be some of her skin beneath them. At some point, he lowered her to the ground, the life all but squeezed out of her. Margaret Ann Pahl was still alive but only moments away from meeting her maker. He took out the weapon that he had carried with him. She was still alive when he began the ritual.

About 7 A.M., hospital worker Wardell Langston heard noise in the general area of the chapel. Then all was quiet until Sister Phyllis, the hospital administrator and the only one with a phone in her room, arrived at the chapel sometime between 7:45 and 7:50 A.M. The chapel doors were unlocked; one stood open.

Sister Margaret Ann likes to get up early and get her work done in the chapel, Sister Phyllis thought.

Phyllis walked over to a front pew. She knelt down and said her morning prayers. A quick glance at her watch told her it was 8 A.M. No hurry. Phyllis said some more prayers.

Fifteen minutes later, Sister Madelyn Marie came down the hallway leading to the chapel. The chapel's organist, she was going to help Sister Margaret Ann get ready for evening services. Madelyn Marie also figured to consult with Father Robinson regarding the music for the Holy Saturday evening Mass. She saw what she thought was a small man in a hurry as he went down the hallway to the exit. Thinking nothing further of it, Madelyn Marie kept walking.

That's when she spied the cloth. It looked more like a pillowcase. She actually couldn't be sure what it was except a cloth of some kind. It had been neatly folded by someone and placed against the wall, just a few feet away from the executive director's office door, which was immediately adjacent to the chapel entrance.

Not thinking twice about it, Madelyn Marie picked it up. Without unfolding it, she entered the chapel and placed it on one of the pews. Then she knelt down in a front pew and began saying her morning prayers.

Where is Sister Margaret Ann? Probably in the sacristy, Madelyn Marie thought.

Madelyn Marie spied the used cleaning cloths on top of the altar. The work to prepare the altar for tonight's service was obviously incomplete. That was odd. Sister Margaret Ann was a perfectionist who did not leave a job half done. Getting up from her pew, Madelyn Marie strode to the sacristy door. She tried the knob; it was locked. That was curious. It was self-locking. Normally it would have been left open when someone was preparing the altar for a service.

Producing a key from her pocket, Madelyn Marie slid it into the lock. Turning gently, the lock disengaged with a click. The Sister of Mercy pushed the door open to a dark room suddenly flooded with light. Walking into the sacristy, she saw at first what she thought was a CPR mannequin on the terrazzo floor. There was no blood.

Bending down to look further, she realized that she was looking at her friend Margaret Ann, and that she had been murdered. It had been a matter of seconds since she had been in the room, but Madelyn Marie knew that life as she'd known it was over. Then she ran out of the sacristy and screamed.

Then, a moment later, she shouted:

"Sister Margaret Ann has been raped!"

Sister Phyllis came running down the aisle, up to the

altar and over to the sacristy door, where she pulled up. Madelyn Marie turned to look at her in shock. Phyllis brushed past her and saw Sister Margaret. She was posed across the room, nearer to the second door. Her underwear and girdle had been pulled down around her ankles. Her habit had been pulled up to her neck. There was a black smudge of blood on her forehead, but very little elsewhere.

"Get help!" Phyllis shouted behind her to Sister Clarisena, who had just come in.

Phyllis helped Madelyn Marie to a pew, and then went back inside the sacristy. Searching desperately for a phone with which to summon help, she found none. Instead, she ventured closer to the body. Phyllis noticed that Margaret Ann's habit was pulled up over her chest. Margaret Ann's face was swollen. A nurse, Phyllis knew that if she was stabbed in the chest and air was sucked out of the body, her face would indeed swell like that.

There were wounds over her heart, quite a few, but surprisingly, very little blood. Most curiously, Margaret Ann's arms were at her sides. Her legs went straight out. Phyllis had already seen quite a few deaths, but none like this. There was weirdness to it all, like something unnatural had been done.

People usually don't die so straight, Phyllis thought.

She had slept in and gotten up at 6:45 A.M., breakfasted quickly by herself on cold cereal, orange juice, and coffee in the nuns' kitchen area, and come back upstairs to do some chores. After that, she relaxed, listened to some rock on the radio, and then decided to take a shower. Sister Kathleen had been in the shower for maybe five minutes, and was just about finishing up, when she overheard a conversation in the hallway between Sister Patricia Ann and one of the other sisters. The shower door was open so that the room didn't steam up. That made her hearing even better.

Sister Patricia said she had just heard a Swift Team call to the chapel. Kathleen thought it might concern Sister Philip, because of her age and medical condition. A few seconds later, a phone rang someplace. There was a pause, the kind of moment that goes on for a lifetime.

"Sister Margaret has been murdered in the chapel," said Patricia, suddenly appearing outside the shower door like the Grim Reaper.

"Go ahead without me," yelled Kathleen, grabbing her towel.

She put on her robe, returned to her room, and dressed quickly, leaving her hair up, and then went directly to the chapel.

Dr. Lincoln Vail was tired. Vail had caught the midnight shift at Mercy Hospital. That sort of figured since he was a second-year resident without much pull. The evening of April 4 into the early hours of April 5 was very busy at the hospital. Vail was a good doctor. He took extensive notes for his morning conference with two colleagues. Vail was in his morning report at 8 A.M. with two other MDs discussing the previous evening's activities when the PA system came alive.

"Emergency, emergency, Swift Team report to the chapel. Repeat, Swift Team report to the chapel!"

Vail was part of the Swift Team, a group of nurses and physicians who responded to medical emergencies within the hospital considered dire. Running down the stairs, he emerged into a rapidly crowding hallway. He saw Sister Kathleen Marie crying and Sister Phyllis Ann comforting her. He entered the sacristy.

"She's already dead," said Dr. Ben Piazza.

Piazza was standing next to the body. He had been walking nearby when he heard the Swift Team alert and responded more swiftly than the Swift Team.

"She may have been raped," Piazza added.

Vail looked down and saw that her girdle and underwear were down around her ankles. Bending down, he held Margaret Ann's wrist. The skin was cold, the pulse, gone. He felt her chest; her heart had stopped beating. Moving back from the body, he noticed the stab wounds over Margaret Ann's heart, then the stab wounds in her neck.

It was at this point that the crime scene was completely compromised. Suddenly a trio of doctors, Dr. Fine, Dr. Howard, and Dr. DeRita, appeared at Vail's side. Then a nurse entered the sacristy. Then two or three of the girls from Respiratory Therapy came in.

"Gloria," said Vail, turning to the nurse. "Cover her with a blanket."

Vail had made the same mistake so many others before him did when they entered the realm of murder. For Vail, Margaret Ann was a dead patient entitled to propriety. But Margaret Ann had forfeited that right when she became a murder victim. Vail's sincere attempt to protect Margaret Ann's modesty transferred a whole lot of fibers to the body that the forensic team would have to sort out later.

* * *

Judy Johnson had a daughter who was in the hospital overnight. Like any good parent, she had stayed with her daughter, to be near her side. Despite what little sleep the hospital couches supplied, by morning she was exhausted. Going down to the cafeteria, she was at the cashier purchasing a wake-up coffee.

"Something's wrong in the chapel!" someone screamed.

Johnson looked over. It was a woman who had just run in from the corridor outside. What happened next was pure mob mentality. Everyone but Johnson ran for the door at once. Johnson waited until the rush died down, long enough to notice a man, about five-six, 140 pounds, light complexion, perhaps Mexican, in his early twenties, curly dark hair, wearing a hospital-type jacket with dark clothing underneath. He stood there with a frightened look on his face. The description, of course, could fit every second worker in the hospital who was Hispanic or light-skinned black.

At about that moment, coming down the connecting passageway to the chapel, was Sister Kathleen. Outside the chapel, Sister Kathleen saw Sister Phyllis in the doorway. There were people crowding around inside.

"What happened, Sister?" Sister Kathleen asked, suddenly feeling anxious.

"Sister Margaret has been murdered and possibly raped," Phyllis replied with a calm she really didn't feel.

"Damn it!" said Kathleen under her breath.

Kathleen ignored several members of the Emergency Medical Team who came running down the chapel aisle, and just kept going. Kathleen came into the narrow room close behind them and saw the body of Sister Margaret Ann on the floor. Father Swiatecki stood to her left. He was uncorking a small vial of olive oil blessed two days before at Holy Thursday's Mass by Bishop Donovan himself.

Since Margaret Ann's birth, one of the changes in the Church dealt with the sacrament of extreme unction. "Extreme," of course, meant the dire circumstances under which the sacrament was given—impending death. "Unction" means oil. Under Vatican II, the sacrament became known as anointing the sick.

Under the old Church rules before Vatican II, the last rites—this included extreme unction, the Holy Eucharist, and penance—were given to those close to death. Vatican II changed that so that the so-called last rites could be commonly given not just to those facing death, but to those who were sick and needed the power of Christ to help them heal. For Margaret Ann, though, it was too late.

"Through this holy anointing, may the Lord in his love and mercy help you with the grace of the Holy Spirit," said Father Swiatecki.

The big priest dabbed his finger quickly on the bottle's neck, getting it wet with the holy oil. Then he made the sign of the cross on the cooling skin of Margaret Ann's forehead. At that moment, the police didn't know it, but they got a big break. For some reason, he took particular care not to touch the bloodstain on her forehead.

Looking up, Father Swiatecki noticed Sister Kathleen.

"Come stand near me," he invited Kathleen.

Doing as Father asked, Kathleen proceeded to step over Margaret Ann's cooling body. She stood next to Swiatecki. He was using the oil to anoint Margaret Ann's hands. He then repeated the ancient prescription meant to remind all Catholics they die with Christ so that they may live again through him.

"May the Lord who frees you from sin, save you and raise you up."

"Amen."

Margaret Ann's life, which began seventy years and 364 days earlier in an Edgerton, Ohio, farmhouse, ended on the cold marble floor of that Toledo church.

Suddenly Father Gerald Robinson, the hospital's head priest, appeared in the chapel. Swiatecki saw him, came and stood over him. Robinson was a stocky, handsome man, but the larger priest menacingly dwarfed him.

"Why did you kill her?" Swiatecki demanded.

Before Robinson could reply, Swiatecki asked for the second time in the presence of witnesses, "Why did you kill her?"

In the cafeteria, thirty-year-old Patrolman Dave Davison and his partner Hank Brackett were eating breakfast. They heard a "Code Blue" over the cafeteria loudspeaker and thought nothing special about it. In Mercy Hospital, codes, as hospital insiders referred to them, were called all the time.

A gangling six-footer with a drooping, Rollie Fingers–type mustache and the ace Oakland Athletic relief pitcher's intense black eyes, Davison was the senior man. Both Davison and Brackett were police officers in District 111—four all African-American housing projects. It was a high-crime area, where most of the criminals were residents preying on their own.

Davison was a real believer in the Atkins Diet before it ever became popular. He was eating bacon and eggs. It was a lot of food and a good deal because the sisters fed the cops at the employee rate. Someplace a telephone rang. A few moments later someone shouted to Davison.

"It's for you!"

"Don't answer," said Brackett. "It'll be work or a female."

The problems for Dave Davison started right there.

Brackett was right, of course. Listening to Brackett and not taking the call would have saved Davison his career and a good part of his life. Unfortunately, Davison literally felt a weight on his chest. It was that damn cumbersome badge he wore. Davison wiped his mouth with a paper napkin, quickly stood up, and strode to the cashier, where someone else handed him a phone.

"Come up to the chapel, there's a dead nun up here!" shouted an anxious female voice.

A dead nun?! Davison thought. After he hung up the phone a nurse ran up to him.

"You've gotta come to the chapel. There's a dead nun!"

"I know," said Davison, taking off out of the cafeteria and into the hospital's labyrinth, Brackett at his heels. *It's got to be a heart attack, maybe a stroke victim*, Davison thought, while his feet ran. Davison realized that the code he had heard earlier was for the nun. A few minutes later, he came through a crowd of people jamming the chapel. He and Brackett fought their way through the crowd of gawkers around the narrow sacristy door.

Once inside, Davison saw people milling around the body. He saw her only from the knees down, the legs bent oddly to the sides. *Some idiot covered her with a hospital sheet.* While it was a respectful gesture, he knew it was an easy way to transfer fibers that would contaminate the evidence. Davison heard the people who had worked on the nun say that she was "dead."

The crime scene is completely blown, he thought, and just as quickly turned to Brackett.

"Rope off the crime scene," he told Brackett, certain he didn't get his sarcasm. Davison looked down.

It could be my own grandmother on that floor, he thought. Davison was not Catholic; his mother was. He had promised her that before she died, he would get baptized. He figured that left him plenty of time, so he hadn't bothered to yet.

He pulled his two-way radio off his belt and flipped it on.

"Ten-four, ten-four, this is Patrolman Davison calling dispatcher."

After a moment, he heard the crackle, then the reply, "Dispatcher here."

"Reporting a homicide at Mercy Hospital Chapel. Requesting homicide detectives, coroner's office, and crime lab all be notified and dispatched."

"Roger, Patrolman Davison, acknowledged."

Davison turned back to the crowd.

"Please come this way."

Davison's job now was to sucker all the people who

surrounded the body to stay so he had a chance to question them. It was important to get their immediate statements before they were contaminated, that is, before they had a chance to talk among themselves about what they had seen and heard, or to make any calls to outside parties.

A few seconds later, the last person was escorted out of the sacristy.

While Brackett went outside to their squad car for some yellow crime scene tape, Davison herded the remaining witnesses, the doctors, nuns, nurses, and hospital workers who had gathered around Margaret Ann's body, into an outside corridor.

"All right, tell me," Davison said to no one in particular, keeping careful to modulate his voice, "who's capable of doing this?"

"It's the priest," someone said.

"They argued," said another person.

A few of the others concurred. Davison took notes of all their statements.

"He liked to shake nuns," another added. "He'd shake the shit out of them."

Davison knew Swiatecki. He was a great big guy, jowly, an alcoholic, a police "groupie." Swiatecki would frequently hang with the cops on duty in the hospital, shoot the breeze, and smoke cigars. The senior priest, Gerald Robinson, a distant man, was also a drinker. He knew the answer before he asked the question, but Davison was a dedicated cop and had to ask it anyway.

Davison asked the witnesses if Robinson was "the priest" they were referring to. They all said yes. Davison jotted all this down in his "supplemental report" that he later submitted to his departmental superiors.

To the beat cop, it was looking pretty good. Within an hour after the commission of the murder of a nun, they had a viable suspect.

CHAPTER 3

Inside Job

Vincent Lewandowski didn't get kicked out of Poland by just anybody. The Franciscan priest had managed to incur the ire of the chancellor of the Austro-Hungarian Empire himself, Otto von Bismarck. That pretty much cut off being a priest on that continent. Faced with ostracism at home or going to America, he chose the latter.

In 1874 when Lewandowski immigrated to Toledo, Ohio, he did what so many immigrants do when they come to America: he reinvented himself by becoming Toledo's first Polish-speaking priest to minister to the city's growing Polish-speaking, Catholic community. Lewandowski served the Polish neighborhoods at opposite ends of the city: in the north, on and around LaGrange Street, "LaGrinka" in Polish; and in the south, on and around Junction and Nebraska Avenues, aka "Kush-wantz."

It didn't take long for the Polish Catholics to get their first combination church and religious school. Christened St. Hedwig, it opened in LaGrinka on October 16, 1875. Six years later in 1881, St. Anthony Parish opened its doors in Kushwantz. As the century turned, the Toledo Polish Catholic community had phenomenal growth.

St. Adalbert's in 1907 was established and then St. Stanislaus in 1908. By then it was obvious that Polish Catholics could wield substantial control over the life of the city and its surrounding community if their political, economic, and religious clout were organized under one banner. The Vatican supplied the banner.

On April 15, 1910, the Catholic Church established the Diocese of Toledo. Encompassing 8,222 square miles, the diocese was, and is, a combination of rural and urban areas stretching out across nineteen counties, including Lucas County. The diocese established three more Polish-speaking churches—the Nativity in 1922; St. Hyacinth in 1927; and Our Lady of Lourdes on Hill Avenue in 1927.

Like any minorities who got smart, the Polish Catholics became a united front with the other Catholics in the city. Even with the urban upheavals of the 1960s, and the "white flight" to the suburbs in the 1970s, in 1980 Toledo had grown to a population of 354,635. One out of every four citizens, fully 25 percent of the city's population, was Catholic. This gave the Diocese of Toledo an incredible amount of influence not just in the police department, but in the entire way that government within Lucas County functioned. The *Toledo Blade* would later describe the Toledo Diocese as a "social service powerhouse—an institution that urged young Catholics to seek careers in public service, including law enforcement."

There were enough nuns present who knew what the protocol was in case of an emergency that *not* to expect one or more to notify the diocese immediately would be naïve. The Toledo Diocese probably knew about Sister Margaret Ann Pahl's murder minutes before the Toledo Police Department homicide detectives did. They certainly knew about it hours ahead of the public and had time to plan on how to deal with the unusual situation of a nun being killed in a sacristy. While the diocese pondered its next actions, the infrastructure of Ohio's justice system had kicked in.

The city of Toledo prosecutor handles misdemeanors and traffic tickets. The Lucas County Prosecutor's Office, of which Toledo city was a part, handled felonies, including murder. Investigating homicides within Toledo city limits was the job of the Toledo Police Department (TPD).

Davison's call for homicide detectives was routed by the police dispatcher to Toledo Police Headquarters, where Detective Sergeant L. Przeslawski assigned Detective Art Marx to "assist the officers at Mercy Hospital on a Code 18."

"Code 18" was police jargon for a homicide.

It was explained to Marx that this was an unusual case—the victim was a Catholic nun. While it somehow seemed likely that someplace in American history a nun had been killed, no one could recall such a case immediately. Marx was told "that the nun had been stabbed to death and possibly sexually assaulted." Because of the possibility of sexual assault, Detective Jodi Deele of the Sex Crimes Squad was also dispatched to assist Marx at the scene. Deele and Marx rendezvoused with evidence technician Steve Bodie at the hospital's old emergency entrance on Twenty-third Street. The time was 8:40 A.M. Sister Phyllis Ann and Sister Kathleen escorted them to the chapel.

So far, everything was going by the book. A homicide had been committed. Detectives and crime scene technicians had been dispatched. The officers on the scene would be debriefed by the detectives. As the beat cops, they would know the hospital and its personnel best. It was also Toledo Police Department standard operating procedure for every police officer to file reports on every person interviewed by him at the crime scene. That included "supplemental reports," which contained detailed interviews with witnesses at the scene.

In his report, Detective Marx noted correctly that after Davison and his partner arrived at the crime scene, "The officers then requested that the scene be cleared and they contacted 212 [headquarters] for assistance. After clearing the scene and contacting 212, the officers interviewed personnel at the scene."

These were the people Davison interviewed at the scene who directly implicated Father Gerald Robinson.

"The names of these individuals are listed in the original crime report and the officers' supplemental reports," Marx continued writing in his report.

Everything was standard operating procedure, and perhaps for the TPD, it was. But it was also at this point that the investigation into Margaret Ann Pahl's murder began its slow, twenty-six-year derailment. The train got off the tracks when Detective Marx failed to note in his report that when he arrived at the scene, he ordered Davison and his partner to leave.

"I argued with Marx about leaving," says Davison passionately. "I looked over at my partner and Brackett gave him a look that said, 'You're not going to win this one, buddy.'"

Davison looked back at Marx.

"They booted us out the door," Davison continues. "It made no sense from an investigative perspective. We knew the people at the hospital. They had already implicated Robinson." Marx wanted them to check out the bus stations for any suspicious characters that looked like they might have just killed a nun. "Just dismissing us like that struck me as bizarre behavior," said Davison.

The police department is a paramilitary organization. Patrolmen follow detectives' orders. Davison and Brackett got back in their Chevy Capri police car that they'd parked outside the hospital. Davison readjusted the .357 Magnum on his belt and they took off to check out the bus stations. When his shift was over, Davison would type up both his primary and supplemental reports, including his interviews at the scene, and submit them to his bosses.

Back in the chapel, Marx and Bodie were processing the crime scene. That meant searching the body and the area around it for anything that might bring some enlightenment. Soon, coroner's investigator Abe Heilman arrived. He took one look at the body and picked up the nearest phone. He called his office to make arrangements to have Margaret Ann Pahl's body taken to the county morgue for autopsy. Marx, meanwhile, was making an examination.

"The body was covered with a white sheet-type of blanket. It was later determined that the body was covered by one of the members of the Swift Team. The blanket was partially removed to check the body for signs of life," he noted in his report.

Common law in the United States is for a physician to officially note time of death in order to supply a death certificate and to move the whole process of death legally forward. Whether homicide or natural, death means you have to do something with the body: autopsy, burial, or cremation. For any of that, you need that death certificate to get the ball rolling.

"After finding no signs of life, the time was noted to be approximately 08:45 hours," Marx continued in the cold-sounding prose of a veteran cop. That was the time of death that would officially be listed on the death certificate.

Marx bent down. He felt the body; cold to the touch. He raised her arm. It fell like it was attached to a rag doll. Rigor mortis, the stiffening of the limbs immediately after death, had not set in yet. That meant she had been dead for a very short time. Examining further, Marx noticed that Margaret Ann's black veil, worn as part of her uniform, was lying under the back of her head with the end of the veil extending out and to the right.

There were visible traces of what appeared to be dried blood on the bridge and tip of her nose. There were also numerous puncture wounds in the right side of her face and neck. The blood that had seeped from these wounds appeared to be still wet and dark in color. Someone had wrapped part of a white altar cloth around Margaret Ann's right forearm. The remaining part of the altar cloth was lying along the right side of the body, extending just below her right knee.

There were several red stains visible on the lower section of the cloth that appeared to be blood. Upon looking closer, Marx saw that there were several punctures in the cloth in the area near the right forearm. It appeared that Margaret Ann's right arm had been resting across the front of her chest when she was stabbed. This could be determined by comparing the punctures in the altar cloth with visible punctures in the dress in the area of the chest.

The right upper arm was extended slightly outward to the right, with the forearm in a horizontal position with the body. The arm formed almost a forty-five-degree angle at the elbow. The hand was lying on the floor, palm up, with the fingers forming a loose fist. There was no visible injury to the right hand. That meant a distinct lack of defensive wounds. Whatever had happened to Margaret Ann, she had not been able to defend herself.

When Margaret Ann had gotten dressed that morning, she had put on a blue jumper knit dress, with a silver cross pinned on the left side. Now the dress had visible red stains down the front that could only be blood. The blood was still wet, the stains concentrated around the left side of the upper chest, just over the heart. Neither Marx nor anyone else at the scene noted anything unusual regarding the punctures.

An examination of Margaret Ann's lower body

showed that both legs extended downward and straight out. They were spread apart at the ankle, about twelve inches apart. Her jumper was down, covering her vagina. Below that, her legs were naked, gray pantyhose and a white elastic panty girdle pulled down and resting around her right ankle. It was that state of undress that had so alarmed Sister Madelyn Marie when she first saw the body that she literally cried "rape." Inventorying the rest of her undergarments, Marx coolly noted that the nun had been wearing a white bra and a blue slip.

Margaret Ann was also wearing blue oxford-type shoes, laces both tied. Some killers take the shoes off and even find ingenious uses for the laces. This guy just left them as is. Margaret Ann's eyeglasses, with their cheap gray plastic frames, were found lying on the floor approximately eight inches from her right hand. The right lens had "what appeared to be smudges of blood."

Bodie was taking photos of Margaret Ann's body when the morgue attendants arrived to take her to the next stop on her journey to the grave. As the attendants lifted her up, Bodie spied a pool of dried blood on the terrazzo floor, under the right side of Margaret Ann's head and shoulders. Bodie bent down to examine the stain closer. It looked oval in shape, about nine inches in diameter.

The body was finally removed at 10:30 A.M. But that made it much easier to minutely search the floor. Sister Margaret Ann was a stickler for spotless ones. The area where her body had lain yielded nothing—no stray cigarette butt, no hairs, no fibers, no spit, no blood, *nothing*. Without one piece of physical evidence pointing in the direction of the killer, it was the kind of case that not only would be difficult to solve, it would be difficult to prosecute.

There was also no evidence Margaret Ann Pahl had been killed someplace else and then transported here. The sacristy itself was the crime scene. Standard operating procedure on homicide investigations is to measure the area where the crime is committed. Marx produced a tape measure and engaged it. The room's dimensions came in at eleven by seventeen feet.

The sacristy had two windows and two entrances. Both doorways were located on the south wall. The first solid oak door entered from the right side of the chapel, in back of the Communion rail that fronted the pews. This door was closed and locked when Margaret Ann was found. A key was needed to unlock this door from the outside, which Sister Madelyn Marie used to get in. Bodie dusted the doorknob for prints. He came up with nothing; same with the door.

The second door to the sacristy had an older type of lock that required a skeleton key. The door was found closed, and unlocked with the skeleton key inserted from the inside of the sacristy. This door led to a narrow passageway that in turn led to the stairwell. Bodie checked the second door. Again, no prints. Whoever the guy was, he had been careful not to leave anything behind. He was either forensically aware or damn lucky.

One of the two windows in the sacristy was located on the north side of the room, facing the parking area for the old morgue. The second window faced Twenty-third Street. Both windows had off-white window shades that

Margaret Ann kept halfway down. While the window shade on the Twenty-third Street window was in the normal position, the window shade on the window overlooking the morgue parking area was pulled all the way down, just below the bottom section of the window. A large wooden armchair that usually sat in front of the window was pushed against the right side of the window shade.

The killer had probably pulled the shade down and put the chair against it to be sure it stayed in place while he went about his cowardly business. The morgue parking area saw a lot of passenger and car traffic.

Marx wrote this in his report:

"It is this investigator's opinion that a stranger to the surroundings in the chapel/sacristy would not normally have the incentive or initiative to lower the window shade to avoid being detected."

That was police speak for an "inside job." Marx was asserting, however well politically, that an insider who knew the chapel and its environs well, especially the sacristy, had committed the murder.

The sacristy was bare of furniture, save for the aforementioned chair, three small wooden utility tables, and two portable kneelers. Normally found on the small table in front of the window, someone had deliberately placed the kneelers in an unusual place under the Twenty-third Street side window. Usually stored in the cabinet behind the table, a cardboard box containing altar decorations and draperies had been placed on a table in front of the storage cabinets. Margaret Ann had moved these items just prior to her murder.

Father Swiatecki came in to check that nothing was missing. He did a quick inventory. It appeared nothing had been stolen or tampered with. Marx wrote in his notes that the light switch was on when Sister Madelyn Marie found the body. While the murder had occurred in the sacristy, the killer might have come through the chapel to commit the crime. Time to check out the chapel.

Lying on top of the altar were assorted boxes of pins that had been placed there by Margaret Ann. A wooden chair, similar to the one found in the sacristy, had been placed in front of the altar. The chair was turned sideways to allow Margaret Ann to stand on it to reach the high draperies behind the altar. The altar cloth that was found wrapped around Margaret Ann's arm had previously been attached with tape to the top of the altar where Margaret Ann had been working.

Searching the pews, on the middle right side, Bodie found a prayer book and small purse. At first, the cops thought they were Margaret Ann's, until Sister Mary Clarisena appeared to claim them as her own. Not so the neatly folded altar cloth. Marx found it in the first pew, left side, at the extreme right end of the chapel. It was exactly where Sister Madelyn Marie had placed it, after finding it lying on the floor in the hall.

Marx gave it to Sister Kathleen. She unfolded it slowly. As she did, it became evident that it was bloodstained. After a few more questions, Marx determined how the cloth had gotten into the pew through Sister Madelyn's actions. He gave it to Bodie for bagging as evidence. When it was brought into headquarters from the crime scene, the TPD would mark, tag, and place it the evidence safe. The crime lab would later examine the cloth and see what they could come up with.

The chapel's highly polished terrazzo floor was pristine. There was absolutely no evidence to indicate that there was any type of struggle at or near the altar when Margaret Ann was working. Plain and simple, the killer had surprised and killed her in the sacristy.

Marx and Bodie then spent some time being escorted through the hospital to Margaret Ann's dorm room. They searched it, finding nothing unusual. Walking back downstairs, retracing Margaret Ann's movements to the sacristy, Marx interviewed the Sisters of Mercy who knew Margaret Ann and had been on the scene when she was discovered.

Sister Madelyn Marie explained how she had found the altar cloth in the hallway outside and placed it on the pew where Bodie found it. Marx asked her why she thought Sister Margaret Ann had been raped. It was a good question, considering that was, after her scream, her first verbalization of what she had seen, or thought she had seen.

"I don't know why I thought that," she answered. "I assumed it from what I heard the others saying." Then, in the kind of cold, unemotional prose common to police reports, Marx wrote, "Sister seemed to become upset . . . that it may have not been a man and that there may have not been a rape."

"It could have been me," she said suddenly. "I have big hands. I could have done it. But I was in my room until after it happened."

Madelyn Marie was suddenly suggesting herself as

a suspect? It didn't make any sense. But she continued with that theme: maybe it was a woman and not a man who had killed Sister Margaret Ann.

"Did you know what they say about nuns? What they do together, when they are *alone*? They will say this is what caused the death."

The sister was clearly implying some sexual link to the crime. None of the interview made any sense. Kathleen's movements prior to the murder were easily accounted for. So why was she "copping" to a crime she clearly could not have committed?

There would be plenty of time afterward to analyze why someone implicates himself in a crime that he clearly could not have committed. The immediate goal was to catch Margaret Ann's murderer. Toward that goal, Marx finished his interview with the nun and left the hospital. He drove to the county morgue and consulted with assistant coroner Dr. Renate Fazekas, who had been assigned to the case.

"She was strangled prior to the stabbing," Fazekas told Marx in his preliminary report. Fazekas's basis for this conclusion was "visible petechia on the face." Petechia is small red or purple spots on the surface of the skin or mucous membranes as the result of tiny hemorrhages of blood vessels. When a person is strangled, petechia of the face is common.

"It appeared the victim was strangled from behind by an individual with large hands," Fazekas also stated to Marx, who noted, "This was the doctor's opinion due to the fact that a rather large bruise was noticed on the back of her neck."

Fazekas, however, cautioned Marx that they couldn't determine the cause of death until a complete autopsy was performed. That, of course, was and is SOP for coroners. As for sexual assault, it was impossible to be determined until the results of the rape kit came in and Margaret Ann's body was completely examined. The rape kit consisted of vaginal swabs, oral swab, rectal swab, fingernail clippings from the left and right hands, hair samples from the skull and pubis, and a blood specimen from Margaret Ann.

The idea was to group and type the blood on each item, and then compare it to the blood taken from Margaret Ann's body. Police forensic specialists would also attempt to determine the presence of sperm in Margaret Ann's vagina, mouth, and/or rectum. Rape could easily be proven if any foreign fluid matched that of a suspect. The coroner would also attempt to determine if there was any flesh or blood under the nails of Margaret Ann that could be compared to the killer's, if and when they caught him.

Fazekas opined to Marx that while it was uncertain until after autopsy how the victim died, it was the doctor's opinion that the victim had probably been strangled prior to being stabbed. That's why there was so little bleeding—when a person's heart stops, she doesn't bleed.

Marx left to continue his investigation.

As the new decade of the 1980s took shape, Toledo was going through profound social and economic changes.

With Japanese cars having successfully challenged and

won the pockets of the American car-buying public with their superior products, cities like Toledo that relied on American auto factory employment for their livelihood saw production slow down. The city's economy plunged.

The Diocese of Toledo was going through changes just like anything else. But one thing they still had were the go-to guys in the TPD. They were the staunch Catholic cops, like Sergeant John Connors, who were called by the diocese when someone charged a priest with sexually abusing a child in their care. That was when the tacit agreement between the TPD and the diocese to protect the priests so accused came into play. Suddenly any criminal charges against the pedophiliac priest would disappear as quickly as the diocese transferred the accused to some remote parish in the county.

None of this would become public until the *Toledo Blade* published an article on July 31, 2005, that said in part, "Over the past 50 years, those sworn to enforce the law and protect children repeatedly have aided and abetted the diocese in covering up sexual abuse by priests, a three-month investigation by *The Blade* shows.

"Beyond past revelations that the diocese quietly moved pedophile priests from parish to parish, *The Blade* investigation shows that at least once a decade—and often more—priests suspected of rape and molestation have been allowed by local authorities to escape the law."

But this was 1980 and the agreement of concealment was still in place. Dr. Lincoln Vail was not a Catholic. He knew little about the religion. But that night, the night after the morning that Margaret Ann Pahl was murdered, he discussed the Swift Team call to the chapel with his wife, Colleen. He told her all about his encounter with the murdered nun.

Colleen took it all in. She had had psychiatric training. More importantly, she had common sense.

"Linc, someone on the inside did it," she told her husband.

CHAPTER 4

The Body Speaks

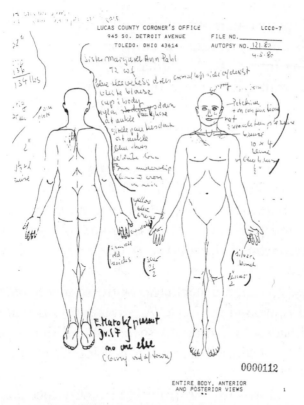

ENTIRE BODY, ANTERIOR
AND POSTERIOR VIEWS   1

Margaret Ann Pahl had made a difference in life by serving her Lord. Now, in death, she had one more chance

to make a difference by serving the state. While her soul was now with her Lord, her body was left on earth as a vessel of that spirit. In the hands of a good pathologist, a dead body can speak volumes. Dr. Renate Fazekas was good at his trade. His job was to help the Sister of Mercy solve a homicide—her own.

The morgue attendant placed her on the ME's table. It was made of cold metal, with channels cut into it. Once the pathologist cut, the channels drained blood off quickly. Before getting to that, Fazekas started with an external examination of Margaret Ann's body.

"The body is that of a 71 year old female weighing 134 pounds and measuring 62" in length," Fazekas began, dictating into a tape recorder nearby. The tape would later be transcribed and turned into the official autopsy report that would be given to police. If a prosecution resulted, it would be introduced at trial as a prosecution exhibit. Fazekas proceeded with what should have been Margaret Ann's last examination by a medical doctor.

"The body is dressed in a blue sleeveless dress. White blouse, blue under slip, white bra, pantyhose, girdle pants, and blue shoes. Pantyhose and girdle pants are gathered around the ankles. A black veil accompanies the body.

"A silver-colored necklace, with a [silver] cross attached is around the neck. A [silver] cross is pinned to the left side of the dress. A silver colored ring is on the 4th finger. Rigidity has not yet developed. Lividity was absent."

Livor mortis or postmortem lividity occurs after death. Blood settles in the lower part of the body, causing a red/purple skin discoloration. Parts of the body in contact with the ground or something else do not show this discoloration, however, because the capillaries are compressed. Lividity being absent on Margaret Ann's body confirmed that she was a "fresh kill," meaning evidence was recent and had not yet deteriorated.

"A 3½" long oblique scar is over the right lower abdomen."

It was an appendectomy scar. Someplace along the line, Margaret Ann had appendicitis and had to get the useless vestige of an organ removed.

"A 1½" long oblique scar is over the medial aspect of the left knee."

Margaret Ann had had an operation to repair the medial ligament of the left knee.

"The teeth are natural."

Suddenly, Fazekas changed direction.

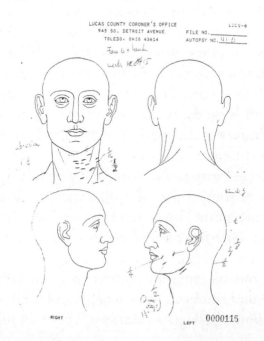

"The body is involved with multiple stab wounds and evidence of strangulation. There are six stabs wounds to the left side of the face. The stab wounds are transverse and oblique [author's note: remember this for later] over the left angle of the mouth and just below the left side of the jaw. The deepest penetration measures 1½"," he dictated.

This was not only major damage, it was major rage. The killer had stabbed the nun so hard, he had gone through the skin of the mouth and into Margaret Ann's jawbone.

"There are fifteen transverse and slightly oblique stab wounds to the left aspect of the neck. The direction of the stab wounds is from front to back. The deepest penetration measures 3"."

Because of the obvious similarities, the ME opined they had been made by the same, unknown instrument.

"There are nine transverse and oblique stab wounds to the left side of the chest, between the left clavicle and nipple line. Two of the stab wounds range in size from ⅛" to ½" in length. They are similar to the above described stab wounds. Some have a slightly irregular outline. The direction of the stab wound is front to back. The deepest penetration measures 3"."

Three inches may not sound like much, but in the case of Margaret Ann Pahl's chest, that meant the sharp instrument penetrated through her chest cavity, right into her heart. If it hadn't stopped beating by then, it most certainly would have immediately. Perhaps it was the very brutality of the crime that caused the ME to miss the most important evidence of Margaret Ann's murder. It was staring him right in the face.

Fazekas's autopsy photographs and diagrams show that the nine stab wounds over Margaret Ann's heart formed the pattern of a cross, tilted slightly to the left. In deference to the ME, the cops had missed it too, and the reason is simple. Who could imagine a priest killing a human being, let alone doing so in such a ritualistic way? It didn't make any sense. Murder never does, but this case was setting a new standard for the unbelievable.

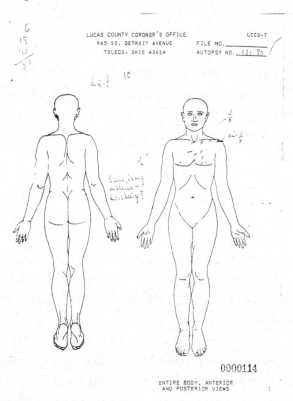

ENTIRE BODY, ANTERIOR
AND POSTERIOR VIEWS

With his external examination complete, Fazekas made the classic pathologist's "Y" incision down the body to examine her internally. Only then would he know the damage that the stabbings had done to her organs.

"The left common carotid artery reveals a rent at the cranial segment. The larynx and trachea reveal three stab wounds. The esophagus is perforated one time. The fourth and fifth cervical vertebrae [in the neck] are each involved with a stab wound. The entire anterior and lateral neck is hemorrhagic."

She had been stabbed hard enough not only to perforate parts of the throat and organs, but some of the stabbings had been hard enough to go through skin, into the spine, and take out two vertebrae. That alone would paralyze someone for life.

"Her left lung had been stabbed twice," the ME continued, "the sternum contains stab wound at the level of the third inner costal space, which extends through the right ventricle, just below the cusps of the pulmonary valve."

The killer got her right in the heart.

Under a section entitled "Evidence of Strangulation," the ME wrote, "Numerous distinct petechias involve the conjunctive of both upper and lower eyelids and the face with the exception of the forehead. Both supra and infraclavicular areas are recently bruised (blue). The area measures 10" x 4". An oblique linear bruise, outlining the necklace, is over the right supra and infraclavicular area."

Margaret Ann had been strangled by *something,* probably large hands that had left the imprint of her necklace in her skin. The assault resulted in a classic symptom of strangulation, the "distinct petechia" or broken blood vessels in the upper face. To finally make the point, the ME concluded:

"Both cornu of the hyoid bone are fractured. The fracture sites are surrounded by hemorrhage."

In a classic strangulation, the hyoid bone of the throat is broken by the killer's increasing and persistent pressure on the throat. This guy had fractured the hyoid bone in two places. Fazekas also noted something else important.

"A 3½" x 2" recent bruise prominently involves the bonily prominent area of the lower cervical and upper thoracic spine, slightly to the right. Within the area are three parallel longitudinal, linear bruises, each measuring 2" in length."

What the ME was describing were inner thigh bruises symptomatic of rape. The rape kit results had also come back as follows:

MICROSCOPIC EXAMINATION:
DEEP VAGINAL SMEAR:
No sperms identified.
VAGINAL SMEAR:
No sperms identified.
ORAL SMEAR
No sperms identified.
RECTAL SMEAR:
No sperms identified.

That pretty much cinched it as a circumstantial case. If the killer had raped her with his penis, it was sheathed. Regardless, there was a complete lack of semen with which to type her assailant. It was possible she had been penetrated by an object other than a penis, but there was nothing inside her vagina, her mouth, or her anus to indicate forced penetration by any sort of object.

In his concluding "Diagnosis," the last one Margaret Ann Pahl would ever get from a doctor, Dr. Fazekas wrote, "Multiple stab wounds (31) to left side of the face, neck and chest, strangulation.

"Opinion: This 71-year-old white female, Sister Margaret Ann Pahl, died of multiple stab wounds to the left side of the face, neck and the chest. There also was evidence of strangulation."

Fazekas was *not* saying she had died from strangulation. Clearly, she was alive when she was stabbed repeatedly. If she wasn't alive, she wouldn't have bled. The stab wounds provided the immediate cause of death. It was the pattern of those stab wounds, not yet detected, that created the most mystery. While it was possible that the cross-shaped pattern of the chest wounds was a chance rather than deliberate occurrence, if you added the altar cloth into the equation, things certainly did get interesting.

Would the killer place the altar cloth over Margaret Ann's chest *by chance*, and then stab her *by chance* in the shape of a cross? Oh, and the killer stabbed her in the sacristy *by chance* on the only day of the year the *consecrated Host*, the body and the blood of Jesus, is there watching the murder from nearby? The mere fact the killer clearly took his time, did his business in a very secluded place, and slipped away without being caught showed that he knew what he was doing and where he was doing it. He could not have escaped without detection had he not known the ins and outs of the hospital and specifically the chapel and its adjacent areas. He was so confident, he left the lights on behind him; he wanted Margaret Ann discovered the way he had left her.

Margaret Ann had either been the victim of some sort of bizarre ritual killing, or the killer was trying to make it *seem* that way to divert attention from him. If the conclusion was the latter, then this was a very clever killer indeed, someone not only capable of eluding detection, but using the public's popular fascination with ritual killing to get away with murder.

With the autopsy completed, the TPD released the body for burial. It was transported to a funeral parlor in Fremont, Ohio, where Margaret Ann was prepared for her final rest. The undertaker drained her body of blood and filled her veins with embalming fluid. Her body was then cleaned up and placed in a habit that her order provided. Finally, the undertaker placed Margaret Ann in a nice wooden coffin.

April 9, 1980

The last time Fremont, Ohio, had been in the news was in 1893, when former president Rutherford B. Hayes died at his Fremont home, Spiegel Grove. Hayes's estate, which included his tomb, was just blocks from St. Bernardine Chapel.

The first time they buried Margaret Ann Pahl, it was as if God was angry. Ominous black clouds appeared overhead. Everyone who was there would remember later that the winds blew hard, pounding at the doors of the chapel. Inside, it was time to say good-bye. Dur-

ing a Catholic funeral, the Church "commends the dead
to God's merciful love and pleads for the forgiveness of
their sins." Through the funeral rites, Christians "offer
worship, praise, and thanksgiving to God for the gift of
a life which has now been returned to God, the author
of life and the hope of the just."

In the Church's book of ritual *The Order of Christian
Funerals,* the first of the three principal components to a
Catholic funeral is the vigil for the deceased, sometimes
referred to as the "wake." It is held at the funeral home
or the church. This had already taken place. Most importantly for Margaret Ann Pahl's right to finally be laid
to rest, the casket, with the lid closed, had already been
placed in the front of the chapel for the second compo-
nent, the funeral liturgy.

Suddenly, the chapel doors burst open. The wind blew
in the dead leaves from the previous fall that someone
had failed to pick up. Quickly, the doors were closed.
The service continued. The Reverend Gerald Robinson
took to the pulpit. If anyone in that chapel thought of
Robinson as the prime suspect, and therefore thought
Robinson was blaspheming before God in conducting a
funeral service for his victim, he didn't show it.

There followed a funeral Mass for Margaret Ann, in
accordance with Church doctrine: "The Mass, the me-
morial of Christ's death and resurrection, is the principal
celebration of the Christian funeral." The Mass included "the liturgy of the Word, the liturgy of the Eucharist,
and the final commendation." The final commendation
is the prayer in which "the community calls upon God's
mercy, commends the deceased into God's hands, and

affirms its belief that those who have died in Christ will share in Christ's victory over death."

The rite of committal, "the final act of the community of faith in caring for the body of its deceased member," concluded the service as Margaret Ann Pahl was, finally, buried. She would have wanted to be remembered for her good works as a Sister of Mercy and acolyte of Catherine McAuley. Instead, her murderer had cheated her out of that legacy. Her new legacy was to be remembered as a murder victim.

Sister Laura Marie Pahl was not too pleased with this occurrence. Laura Marie was Margaret Ann's sister. She not only was at her sister's funeral, she lived at the St. Bernadine Retirement home in Fremont. She, too, had become a Sister of Mercy, emulating her big "sis." While the TPD figured Laura Marie Pahl probably had no information regarding her sister's murder, there was always the chance she did. The vast majority of murders are committed by people who know, sometimes intimately, the person they are murdering. The questions had to be asked. And so Sister Laura Marie Pahl had come to Mercy Hospital after the funeral, where she met with TPD Detective Peter Brook in the convent community room at the hospital.

"Did Sister Margaret have any enemies?" Detective Brook asked. "Anyone who had a vendetta against her?"

"In January, there had been a family get-together in Edgerton," the old nun answered. "Margaret Ann told me that she and the other sisters at the hospital had seen a black man hanging around the chapel area. The sisters were told [presumably by Sister Phyllis] not to go to the chapel alone. They didn't want the sisters to confront this man alone."

There also seemed to be a power struggle between Sister Kathleen Marie and Sister Phyllis for the top job at Mercy Hospital. Margaret Ann was getting tuckered out from all of it.

"Sister Margaret Ann, during the last six months, had talked about leaving and retiring from the hospital. She was a very quiet person. She seemed very contented with her job in the chapel."

Brook asked the required question of every homicide detective from Maine to Florida and California to Buffalo. Was there anyone she knew of who wanted her sister dead?

"No," she answered, "no one that I knew of had a vendetta against her."

Brook produced an evidence envelope and opened it. Carefully, he took out Margaret Ann's belongings and placed them on the institutional table for her sister. Sorting through the stuff, Laura Marie told Brook, "Something's missing."

"What?"

"My sister had *two* watches."

That was consistent with Margaret Ann's compulsive personality. Marx had already noted she had two different kinds of alarm clocks in her room. In this case, the missing watch was a Bulova that she had purchased at Neumann's Jewelers, at 325 Huron Street in downtown Toledo.

"It was small, silver, with a round face and easy to read numerals. It cost $48," Laura Marie continued.

Looking through his notes, the detective saw that among Margaret Ann's possessions recovered from her room was a receipt for the watch from said jeweler. A police alert would be put out to pawnshops in case someone tried to pawn it. Until it was recovered, it had to be assumed that it was stolen. If no one in the convent had stolen it—always a possibility but not likely—then it had to be in the murderer's possession. If that were the case, the killer was a guy who liked having a souvenir of his kill. It would also be a nice piece of direct evidence for the prosecution to produce in court if they could recover it.

The city of Toledo had been galvanized by Margaret Ann's murder. Citizens wanted the killer caught. Paranoia ran rampant. Toledo's citizens began informing on their neighbors.

Everyone began to look for the man who had killed the nun. The urban myth of the mysterious and suspicious black/Mexican/dark-skinned man reared its ugly head once again. People came forward from all parts of the city and beyond to say that prior to/on the day of/ just after the murder, in the shadows of the hospital/the surrounding neighborhood/the city of Candiotti miles away, there was lurking a mysterious and suspicious black/Mexican/dark-skinned man.

A whole lot of scared white people said it was the black guy "over there," as if a white "bad guy" couldn't be capable of such brutality. Few of the TPD files show a name attached to any of these "suspects." In those cases where they were named, the names have been blacked out because police cleared them of all participation in the homicide. What it does show clearly is racist paranoia. The Toledo cops had to deal with every nut, freak, and schizophrenic that came out of the woodwork to claim knowledge either of the killing or of the person who had done it.

Some of them were classic. Psychic Beverly Holmes called the TPD from nearby Maumee, Ohio. Detective Matt Holbrook took the call.

"I'm calling to offer my services in the Pahl case. I'm a psychic," she told Holbrook, who was taking careful notes. "I've helped the FBI."

"So what do you know?" Holbrook asked.

"A white male from Delaware. I'm not sure if that is the state he is from or the street he lives on."

"Go on."

"The victim knew him. He was carrying a grocery sack and at times flowers which means he is a delivery boy. This person knows music and plays a strung instrument. He has a mental history, caused by the way he was treated by his parents. He is a negative person."

"Anything else?" Holbrook asked politely.

"No."

Hanging up, Holbrook wrote in his notes, "This person appears to have no knowledge of the case whatsoever."

Delaware? One of the more interesting "tips" came from Pat Logston, a schoolteacher at St. Hyacinth. Her husband was the Swanton postmaster. It seemed that Logston had had a dream that was so disturbing, she contacted the Swanton Police Department. She was interviewed by Chief Dave McAuley, who later passed along the information to the Toledo PD.

In her dream, Logston saw a suspect in the Mercy Hospital homicide. She described him as a little fat man about forty years old, who was a cook. She dreamed about the little fat man for several nights in a row. He cooked in large pots. She also dreamed that his name was Caryl Dennis. To the best of anyone's knowledge, no one looking like Lou Costello, or having the famous and rare first name belonging to the legendary California convict Caryl Chessman, was involved in the case.

At 10:45 A.M., on April 18, 1980, evidence technician Shirley Sparks delivered a letter addressed to "Art Marx, Toledo Police Homicide Investigation." Upon opening it, the detective noticed that it was from an anonymous source and concerned the Pahl homicide. He attempted to protect the letter for fingerprints; he had touched only the top of it. He immediately notified his lieutenant, William Kina, and captain, James Navarre, that he'd received an anonymous letter with information regarding the Pahl homicide.

Mindful of the chain of custody necessary for a conviction, Kina asked for Sparks to dust the letter for prints and then put it with the other evidence logged into the property room. Steve Bodie came to the Homicide Desk per Marx's request to process the letter. At 11:30 A.M. Bodie took possession of it.

Here's what the letter said:

> *Here's a tip on the Mercy hospital nun murder:*
> *Try [name blacked out by police].*

*he has a perverse hate for the Catholic Church
and especially nuns (a bitter and imbalanced ex-
Catholic himself)*
*he's very sick and needs help—a psychopath with
a great potential for violence*
he's a woman hater—also sexually deviant
he's into devil worship
*Many times, he has "jokingly" threatened exactly
this type of crime*
*I hope you can help him and stop this before it
happens again—it's in your hands!*

There is nothing in the police files that points to the identity of the person whose name is blacked out in the police report. Nor is there anything in the files indicating that police took the note any more seriously than the psychic and the dreamer. Marx, though, had a better idea than the psychic and the dreamer. He would interview the priest, Father Gerald Robinson. But he wasn't the only one thinking about him. Robinson was very much on the minds of the people back at Mercy Hospital.

To say that the place had been shaken up would be putting it mildly. Murder not only ripples through generations, it ripples through the society in which it has been committed. For those working in Mercy Hospital, they had to come to work knowing a human life had been deliberately taken in a place dedicated to saving life. It was an irony that produced not only sadness, but anger.

"The staff at the hospital *knew*," Dave Davison says

bluntly. "Every time we went in there to question people, the hospital workers would tell me off the record, 'Robinson pounded on nuns.' But no one would give a statement on record saying that. The hospital workers were afraid to talk openly. They told me, 'You talk, you're fired.'

"The order came from on high."

CHAPTER 5

An American First

What was unfolding in Toledo, Ohio, in April 1980 was a first in American criminal law, yet it came in under the national news radar.

The country was concerned with freeing American hostages in Iran being held by Islamic fundamentalists at the U.S. embassy. Who cared what happened in a northern backwater town? With only three television networks, Toledo was a lowly network affiliate that rarely saw national coverage. Yet the Toledo cops were dipping their feet into history.

No priest had ever been charged, let alone convicted, of murdering a nun in the United States. Even going back to colonial times in the seventeenth and early eighteenth centuries, there are no recorded instances of such a bizarre event. When priests do show up in pamphlets of colonial accounts of crimes, they appear as pristine father confessors to the murderers in question. As the United States spread across the continent in the nineteenth century, priests found themselves in all kinds of situations on the American frontier. Their brethren back east ministered to the poor and infirm in northern tenements.

In the twentieth century, a new element entered the mix that would eventually complicate the Pahl case. Motion pictures would forevermore color the public view of priests as honest, virtuous, and godly men, making it that much more difficult to believe any one of them could be capable of committing murder. When motion pictures became the chief disseminators of priestly values, it wasn't just Catholics who thought of priests this way, it was everyone who went to the movies.

Whether a Methodist child in Oregon, an Episcopalian tomboy in Arizona, a Jewish kid in Brooklyn, or an agnostic in Toledo, they all saw the same movies about priests and thought of them in the same way. Television's introduction to the general public in 1948 and the subsequent videotapes and DVDs of these same films shaped public opinion about priests for generations, more than real-life events. They still do. The reason is, the men who directed these films weren't the kind of film directors who relied on kinetic cutting, special effects, graphic bloodletting, sadism, or nihilism.

They were, for better or worse, directors out to entertain. Unlike others, their goal was not social realism. On the contrary, their job was to create a fantasy, in this instance regarding priests, to be consumed by the masses. The three directors who would have the most profound influence on how generations to come looked at priests were Michael Curtiz, who made his first film in Hungary in 1912 and knew how to use a camera; Norman Taurog, a journeyman film director who would take his game to the highest plane; and Leo McCarey, who would have, perhaps, the most influence on how future generations thought of priests.

More than any other movie studio in the 1930s, Warner Bros. used priests as major characters in its classic gangster films. In all of them, the tough-guy priest was a key character. The idea was to contrast the saintliness of the priest, usually played by Pat O'Brien, with the evil of the gangster, usually Jimmy Cagney. Of course, in the end, saintliness always won. This theme reached its zenith with Michael Curtiz's *Angels with Dirty Faces* (1938). With a script doctored by the great screenwriters Ben Hecht and Charles MacArthur, Curtiz produced a hit movie that became the apotheosis of the godly priest. The plot went something like this.

Rocky Sullivan (Cagney) and Jerry Connelly (O'Brien) were tough kids who grew up together in Hell's Kitchen, the toughest part of New York City. Rocky gets sent to reform school, where he learns how to be a first-class criminal. Jerry, who had escaped from the law, goes straight and becomes a priest. As adults, they reunite in the old neighborhood. Jerry works with the children (the Dead End Kids) who, like he and Rocky, could end up on either side of the law.

Rocky returns looking for a safe place to stay till he can get back into his old racketeering organization, something Jerry is determined to prevent. When Rocky is convicted of murder and sent to the chair, Jerry visits him right before his execution. He pleads with his old friend to "turn yellow" when he dies. This way, the Dead End Kids won't want to emulate him. Rocky turns his old friend down, finishes his last meal, and is escorted on the last mile.

As he walks to his death, Cagney performs a remarkable acting feat, suddenly going from tough, hard-as-nails gangster to whimpering coward as he's strapped in the chair. Then the electricity is turned on and he is no more. When the Dead End Kids read of their idol "turning yellow," they realize the criminal life is not for them and decide to go straight forever.

Father Pat O'Brien has just won their souls and ours. Priests are only capable of helping young boys out chastely.

Hollywood never does anything in "ones." That same year, 1938, another film about a priest didn't become a hit—it became a *massive* hit and a classic. In an era where people paid a dime to see a movie, *Boys Town* (1938) took in millions of dollars. It told the dramatic tale of the legendary Father Edward J. Flanagan, the founder of Boys Town, who coined the phrase, "There is no such thing as a bad boy."

Despite the sentimental nature of the material, Dore Schary's story and script emphasized the humanity in Flanagan's character. Journeyman director Norman Taurog hit a home run before even getting to the set when he cast the one actor who could perform a sentimental part unsentimentally—Spencer Tracy. Tracy didn't have a sentimental bone in his body. He made you believe in the two-fisted but always virtuous priest and won the 1938 Best Actor Oscar for his performance.

Then in 1944, Leo McCarey made film history by humanizing the rapidly developing archetype of the virtuous priest. A silent film director, McCarey specialized in comedies. It was McCarey who had teamed Stan Laurel and Oliver Hardy for the first time on screen. Effortlessly bridging into directing sound films, in the 1930s he directed such disparate screen comedians as the Marx Brothers and Cary Grant.

In 1944 at forty-six years of age, McCarey was at the height of his creative powers. He decided to use everything he had learned along the way to write, direct, and produce a film that would reduce its audience to crying tears of laughter one moment and flat-out tears of sentiment the next. McCarey's idea was to refine the American priest myth to its ultimate conclusion. He called it *Going My Way*, and his premise was simple.

Father Chuck O'Malley, a young, golf-playing, happy-go-lucky priest, is sent by the New York Archdiocese to a broke Roman Catholic parish in the slums of Manhattan. There, O'Malley clashes with crusty Father Fitzgibbon, an old-school Catholic priest with a secret heart of gold. Throw in an extraneous love plot where O'Malley plays cupid and sings a few songs, and pretty soon, everything works out.

Working through his own devices and of course the grace of God, Father O'Malley saves the parish; reunites Fitzgibbon with his beloved Irish mother flown over especially from the ol' Sod; gets Romeo and Juliet together, and then moves on like the benevolent angel he really is.

That was the script McCarey the screenwriter wrote. Then McCarey the director took over. To play O'Malley, the key role, he cast popular radio crooner and light screen comedian Bing Crosby. Besides the classic *Road* movies he did with his friend and golf partner Bob Hope, Crosby's other films always made money. He had an easy screen presence. You just trusted him, even when he was duping Hope in the *Road* movies. So perhaps it was natural, then, that McCarey, who understood human nature better than most directors, decided to cast the scene-stealing character actor Barry Fitzgerald as Father Fitzgibbon.

On set, the two leads clashed, just like their characters. It made their screen scenes that much more real. When the time came for each to show the other chaste, priestly devotion, their bickering with each other made their acting that much more compelling to watch. Most importantly, Crosby and Fitzgerald's performances, as the smart young priest and the wise, crusty older priest, both godly men, became the public's perception of who and what priests were until almost the end of the millennium.

McCarey's film was a huge, huge (did I say huge?) hit. It topped the year's box office, but in the Pacific Northwest, it was even bigger. Bing Crosby came from Spokane, Washington, and the film played particularly well in Washington and Oregon. Years later Beulah Rose, who along with her husband George "Bud" Rose operated movie theaters in Milton and Freewater, Oregon, would remember that the film played there for a very, very long time, and with good reason.

Going My Way made Hollywood history when McCarey became the first person to win three Oscars for the same picture as writer, director, and producer. But more important to the public that relates better to the stars, Bing Crosby trumped his good friend Bob Hope by taking home the Oscar for Best Actor.

Behind the scenes was a different matter.

Gary Crosby, Bing's eldest of four sons by his first wife, actress/singer Dixie Lee, would later write in his 1984 book, *Going My Own Way,* that his father was abusing his four kids while playing Father O'Malley. That made Crosby's Best Actor Oscar a well-deserved award. Costar Barry Fitzgerald had actually been nominated in both Best Supporting Actor and Best Actor categories because of a nominations anomaly. Fitzgerald won the Best Supporting Actor award.

Father O'Malley proved so popular a character that McCarey, in the best Hollywood tradition of ripping yourself off, immediately penned and directed a sequel, *The Bells of St. Mary's* (1945). This time Father O'Malley (Crosby) winds up at some cool inner city Catholic school where he meets the gorgeous and chaste Sister Mary Benedict (Ingrid Bergman). Once more, McCarey had a hit, and Father O'Malley went straight into the Zeitgeist.

So deeply was this impression of the "good" priest imprinted on the American subconsciousness that Francis Ford Coppola paid homage to it in *The Godfather* (1972). In the scene when Michael (Al Pacino) is on the phone and finds out that his father has been shot, behind him is the Radio City Music Hall marquee. Emblazoned on it in bright red neon is *The Bells of St. Mary's.*

As the 1970s developed, priests in fiction and film became more complex, guilt-ridden characters who find themselves up against satanic forces. While the theme was different, the priests still acted like everyone expected priests to act. In 1971 William Peter Blatty had a huge literary and popular hit with his novel *The Exorcist*. It told the story of a tormented priest who finds redemption exorcising a demon from a young girl. Among other things, the book featured a very dramatic ritual killing.

The 1973 film version became nothing less than a popular phenomenon. Director William Friedkin, an action director who knew character, made sure to put in enough stultifying shocks to grab repeat audiences. It scared the crap out of people when fourteen-year-old Linda Blair's head swiveled 360 degrees and out of her mouth came Oscar-nominated actress Mercedes McCambridge's voice. People screamed in fear.

The public interest in those who would mock the Church and shake it to the ground reached its apex in the most popular, frightening, and influential film featuring satanic worship and ritualistic killing, 1976's *The Omen* (forget the 2006 remake). The plot, once again, is simple.

In David Seltzer's totally believable script, a secret cabal of Satan worshippers mock Catholicism in all kinds of ways, not the least of which is killing at birth the child of the American ambassador to the Court of St. James (Gregory Peck), and then substituting Satan's spawn in its place. That he just happens to be a nice little dark-haired boy named Damien, helped make the story believable, including the ritualistic killings of said baby, a courageous Catholic priest, and a crusading though eccentric reporter. What really sold it was that under Damien's dark hair was the sign of the Devil, "666," a reference to Revelations 13:16 through 13:18.

Except, of course, it is not true. From the Book of Revelation:

Rev. 13:16. "And he causeth all, both small and great, rich and poor, free and bond, to receive a mark in their right hand, or in their foreheads."

Rev. 13:17. "And that no man might buy or sell, save he that had the mark, or the name of the beast, or the number of his name."

Rev. 13:18. "Here is wisdom. Let him that hath understanding count the number of the beast: for it is the number of a man; and his number is *Six hundred threescore and six.*"

The number 666 is the mark of the "Beast" not Satan. Satan, however, sells better than the Beast. The public bought this stuff hook, line, and sinker. People lined streets in Manhattan in the middle of the winter of 1973 to see *The Exorcist*. *The Omen*? Only five other films made more money in 1976, including *Rocky* at number one.

Cut to Toledo, 1980. Thanks to the media, ritualistic killing was still very much on the public's mind. Anyone with a motive could exploit those fears. As for how the public thought of priests, Father O'Malley was still the template. Priests might be guilt-ridden, like *The Exorcist*'s Father Damien, but they were still thought of as men of God who simply repress their emotions in order to do God's work.

As for pedophilia, most Americans in 1980 had never even heard of the word, let alone understood its meaning. Even if they had, no one could imagine Crosby or Fitzgerald sodomizing a little altar boy. Priests being involved in ritualized murder? That was film and fiction.

To believe anything else would make you insane. Inside the Diocese of Toledo, it was another matter entirely.

No priest alive believed in any of that crap, least of all Mercy Hospital's second chaplain, Father Jerome Swiatecki. Swiatecki might have been destroying his liver with all the booze he drank, but his commitment to the Church was unwavering, and more so to his parishioners. He didn't countenance sexual abuse, by anybody. But he was realist enough to know exactly how the Church dealt with such matters.

Inside the Church, priestly pedophilia was old news. It could be an altar boy, the young daughter of a parishioner, anyone they had power over. Some priests sexually abused those in their charge. That was a fact. As for protection, in the true sense of the word, the Diocese of Toledo had struck deals with the go-to guys within the TPD as far back as 1959. To call the agreement between the Diocese of Toledo and the TPD a conspiracy, though, would be giving it more merit than it deserves.

This wasn't a conspiracy in the classic sense of the word. It wasn't as if the diocese and the cops had regular meetings to decide what to do, just in case. It was more an irregular policy that developed along the way, based upon the movie premise that a Catholic priest could never commit a felony.

If a priest got caught sodomizing an altar boy, every effort was made to stop charges from being pressed and to keep the police out of it. To protect the sodomizer, the diocese would reassign him to the next parish . . . and the next . . . and the next. If he actually got caught doing something publicly, like soliciting homosexual sex, the diocese called the go-to guys and the priest was released into the custody of the diocese, which reassigned him to the next parish . . . and the next . . . and the next.

Both institutions, the TPD and the diocese, feared their waning influence. Perhaps it was New Age philosophies; perhaps it was the lure of other religions, or simply assimilation by Polish Catholics. Whatever it was, fewer people were being raised like Margaret Pahl to regularly take the sacraments. It was easy for souls to be corrupted.

The TPD cops took their lives in their hands every time they went out on the street. Bulletproof vests were not common street equipment, but were usually reserved for SWAT teams, making beat cops like Dave Davison that much more vulnerable to a bullet to the torso. In such an environment, the Church was looked at as the ultimate stabilizing influence.

Instead, what had really occurred was that the souls of the Toledo Diocese and the TPD had been corrupted enough that it wasn't too far of a stretch to cover up a murder next. Covering up a murder, though, was truly unknown territory, even for a diocese skilled at manipulating civil authority, and a police department more than willing to acquiesce. In the diocese's favor was that the media had done part of their job—the very idea of a priest killing a nun was odious, let alone the way it was done.

Aware it was a high-profile case, the TPD invited Father Gerald Robinson in for a little chat. On April 18, 1980, at 8 P.M., Father Robinson showed up at police headquarters to be interviewed by Art Marx and his lieutenant, Bill Kina. Accompanying Father Robinson was Father Swiatecki, who was functioning under diocese orders as the former's escort. While Swiatecki stayed outside in a waiting area, Father Robinson was ushered into an interrogation room with institutional furniture. It smelled like most interrogation rooms from stale cigarette smoke, coffee, sweat, and something else that was hard to define. Following then current procedure, the interview with Robinson was not recorded.

Like most cops going into a situation like this, Kina and Marx hoped for a confession. Their job was to find a way to pierce the priest's psychic armor and get him to trip up on some important detail. If they could do that they would build on it. With Kina playing the part of "good cop," leaving Marx the better role as the villainous "bad cop," they peppered the priest with questions, trying to trip him up on essential details. Finally, feeling the pressure, Father Robinson confessed that shortly after the murder, he himself heard the confession from the man who killed Sister Margaret Ann! He could not violate the sanctity of the confessional by telling the police what the man said.

Marx's response might have been cynical had he known that Robinson had just recited the plot of the 1953 Hitchcock film *I Confess*. In that film a priest played by Montgomery Clift hears the confession of his church's caretaker. The caretaker confesses that he just committed murder. The difference is that in the film, Clift refused to violate the confessional's sanctity, even when circumstantial evidence pointed to his own guilt. Monte had more ethics than Jerry.

Without referencing the film, Marx pointed out that Robinson had already violated the confessional's sanctity by even mentioning his conversation with the alleged murderer. What he was really saying to the priest was, *I don't buy that Father O'Malley crap!* Robinson's response was to admit he lied, but only because he didn't know what to do to stop the cops from pressuring him.

The cops pressured him for four hours, and the guy was running down. What they still didn't have was any physical evidence tying the priest to the nun's murder. The easiest way to do that was to get a suspect to voluntarily sign away his constitutional rights and let the detectives search his home. At first glance, a suspect would have to be out of his mind to sign such a document. After all, you are signing away the right to challenge the results of the search in court. If anything incriminating is found, implicating you in a murder case, the state of Ohio has the death penalty.

You could fry.

Surprisingly, the innocent and the guilty sign away this right with frequency. The innocent are naïve. They believe they have nothing to fear and agree to cooperate. After all, all the people in prison are guilty, aren't they? The guilty agree in order to look innocent, especially if they have disposed of any evidence. What, then, is there to fear? Many of the guilty can even beat a lie detector. Having no conscience, sociopaths see nothing wrong with having committed murder. Though they are lying freely, the machine will say they are telling the truth.

Father Robinson was tired. Forget being "interviewed," he had been under interrogation for four hours. Perhaps his judgment was impaired by fatigue or stress. Whatever it was, Marx produced a feat of legerdemain. Innocent or guilty, Reverend Gerald Robinson signed a document Marx presented to him: a "Waiver of Search

Warrant" that "allowed members of the Toledo Police Department, to wit Detective Arthur Marx, to search my living quarters at Mercy Hospital, for a weapon, clothing or cloth materials that might contain blood, and/or any other evidence that might prove to be connected with the death of Sister Margaret Ann Pahl."

The next paragraph was actually the most powerful legally in the document. It was Robinson's last chance to back out.

"I also understand that I have a constitutional right to refuse to have my quarters searched, and there have been no threat or promises made to me, and that I am giving permission free and voluntarily."

Robinson signed it. It was witnessed, "Detective Arthur Marx." Thus did Robinson allow Marx and the state of Ohio the opportunity to legally search his apartment for literally anything that could tie him to Sister Margaret Ann Pahl's murder.

CHAPTER 6

The Fixers and the Smoking Gun

On the morning of April 19, 1980, Detective Arthur Marx went to Reverend Gerald Robinson's apartment adjacent to Mercy Hospital. Father Robinson was home. Marx was accompanied by another TPD detective and Tom Ross, an investigator for the Lucas County Prosecutor's Office. If they found enough evidence to prosecute, it was Ross's office that had jurisdiction.

There really is an art to conducting a good search. The detective has to be aware of how something, however common in a household, can be used at the crime scene as the murder weapon. He also needs to have physical latitude to poke into as many nooks and crannies as a residence has, and know that if he finds something that implicates the suspect, the court won't throw it out on a constitutional technicality That's why cops try to get the judges who sign search warrants to give them a Grand Canyon's worth of leeway in searching a suspect's home.

It soon became apparent that this was not going to be a difficult search. Robinson's quarters were only two small rooms. Located on the second floor of the dormitory wing, Robinson's digs were right next to an exit door, giving the priest easy access to the stairway and therefore the hospital.

If Robinson was the murderer, the immediate question was what he had been wearing at the time he committed the crime. It was only logical to assume that since he had duties in the hospital that morning, Robinson had worn his priestly cassock. That would have made an interesting scene: after Robinson committed the murder, running through the stairway with cassock flying. On the other hand, that was the type of thing people would notice. The cops noticed that the priest's cassock had a dark stain on it. They asked Robinson how it had gotten there.

"It's a gravy stain," Robinson answered. "It's not blood," insisted the priest.

He was but a poor servant of the Lord, with only one cassock. He had given his life to the Church. Take it away and he had no vestments. How could a priest be a priest without his vestments? The cops took it anyway. If the cassock came back positive for Margaret Ann Pahl's blood, it would be worth the inconvenience to Father Robinson's parishioners. They also took a pair of shoes that Robinson said he had worn the day of the murder.

In the medicine cabinet, they found a bottle of Valium, a commonly prescribed medication for anxiety. The prescription date was April 5, 1980, the day of the murder. The cops had to wonder if perhaps Robinson felt some acute anxiety that day and decided to deal with it chemically. They confiscated the Valium bottle too.

They rummaged through the priest's battered wooden desk and found what would later be described in the Toledo Regional Crime Laboratory report as "Exhibit 1—Saber Style Letter opener (8½")." It had a curved blade like a real saber, attached to a medallion and above that a Roman-style faux gold filigreed handle. Realizing that the pointed end of the letter opener could have been used to inflict the wounds on Margaret Ann's body, they bagged it as evidence. The lab would test it for blood and prints. Of course, being that it was Robinson's, it would make no difference if his prints were on it. Blood was another matter.

Later that afternoon, Robinson returned to police headquarters, accompanied by Father Swiatecki. In another masterful feat of persuasion, the cops got Robinson to agree to a lie detector test. The priest, who seemed to be doing everything he could to put himself in the electric chair, was brought into a room where the polygraph operator, Lieutenant James Wiegand, had already set up his equipment. Standard operating procedure in the Toledo Police Department, and every other police department in the country worth its salt, was for the polygraph operator to chat for a few minutes before the test with the subject. Wiegand's speech went something like this:

"Hi, my name is Lieutenant Wiegand and I'm a polygraph operator for the TPD. A polygraph is just a series of measurements. We use pneumographic tubes to measure respiration. Then there are two plates to record galvanic skin responses. As you can see, there's a blood pressure cuff that will record blood pressure and pulse as we proceed through the questions."

What the operator was doing was tapping into Gerald Robinson's autonomic nervous system. There, Robinson has no physical control over his responses to a series of questions designed to test his knowledge of the event in question, in this case the Pahl murder. Questions that make him want to lie will create a sense of emergency to his psychological well-being. The fear of being found out in a lie, in turn, causes the sympathetic part of the autonomic nervous system to respond, which the machine records as "deception," or put more simply, lying.

Most cops tend to rely on the machine much too much, especially considering the results are not admissible in court precisely because the science it is based on is theory and not fact. The proven fact that a sociopath can beat the machine shows that it is not infallible. Justice still depends on "reasonable doubt," not, "It looks like he's lying and therefore he's guilty." However, as an investigative tool, the machine can be invaluable.

If someone flunks a lie test, it points the finger of suspicion at him. It makes the cops look at him with more intensity. It makes detectives work that much harder to find hard evidence of guilt. It was with that hope that Kina and Marx departed while Wiegand produced a form for Father Robinson to sign.

"You have the right to remain silent," Wiegand read.

"Anything you say can and will be used against you in a court of law. You have the right to the presence of an attorney. If you cannot afford one, one will be appointed for you by the court. Do you understand these rights as I have read them to you?"

"Yes," Reverend Gerald Robinson answered, and signed away his constitutional right to have an attorney present while Wiegand questioned him.

Wiegand hooked him up to the machine in the aforementioned manner, and Wiegand went about asking him innocuous biographical questions. The idea was to get a baseline reading and have Robinson settle down for the real stuff. That took about twenty minutes, at which time Wiegand began the real questions about Robinson's involvement in the homicide of Sister Margaret Ann Pahl.

Most of the questions had to do with where he was at key points in the murder timeline the police had constructed. Near the end of the session, Wiegand asked Robinson if he knew anyone who wanted to kill Margaret Ann Pahl. Robinson replied that he knew of no one. Wiegand's response was to ask him why anyone would have wanted to kill her.

"She had a dominant personality," Father Robinson replied.

"She was a dominant woman," Robinson reiterated, almost nonchalantly.

Robinson had just unknowingly supplied cops with what to that point had been missing: a possible motive for the crime. While motive is not necessary to convict, it helps if the killer has a reason to kill the decedent, and you can convince a jury of that. If Robinson felt Sister Margaret Ann had a "dominant personality," one that he found threatening, well, murders have been committed for less.

After the interview was over, Robinson was unhooked from all the doodads, and the cops got him something to eat. Back in the polygraph room, Wiegand went over the results of the lie detector test. Filling out his report for Marx and Kina, he noted that based upon the results of Robinson's polygraph, "It is the opinion of this polygraph examiner that truthfulness could not be verified. Deception was indicated on relevant questions concerning the murder of Sister Margaret Ann Pahl."

It's interesting how many different ways cops can write in reports that a suspect is lying through his teeth and make it sound almost like a compliment. Informed of the results of the lie detector test, Marx and Kina figured they had the priest. While it would take a while to get the analysis of the letter opener, it seemed logical that it could be the murder weapon. Armed with all that, the cops had a lot to pressure Robinson into a real confession.

Robinson found himself in an interview room once again at police headquarters with Marx and Kina. It was Father Gerald Robinson's darkest hour. Just as their interview was getting started, there was a sharp knock at the door. The guy who threw it open looked like he was John Wayne charging the Indians in a John Ford Western, only this was more like an episode of Rod Serling's *The Twilight Zone*.

Deputy Chief Ray Vetter cut an imposing figure. He looked like a Roman centurion, well-built and broad-shouldered, with wavy black hair. Vetter was in charge of investigations for the TPD. Not only was his usual style not to interrupt an interrogation, no one could recall the last time he had walked into a police interrogation room where the prime suspect in a murder sat, about to be given a new asshole by two determined cops.

Everyone knew Ray Vetter to be a devout Roman Catholic who wore his religion on his sleeve. Schooled at a private Catholic school, he believed the seven holy sacraments were sacrosanct. He had six kids, and all of them had been born at Mercy Hospital. He knew the place well. It therefore wasn't terribly surprising that the man who strode in behind Vetter wore a purple-trimmed black cassock with purple sash for all occasions, including police interrogations.

It was probably another first, the first time in American history that a monsignor of the Catholic Church interrupted a police interrogation. Monsignor Jerome Schmit was one of Ray Vetter's best buddies. Schmit had attained the high ecclesiastical title of monsignor for his previous good works. Yet his presence in that room was closer to the way "monsignor" is defined in the *Devil's Dictionary*: "A high ecclesiastical title of which the Founder of our religion overlooked the advantages." A popular Toledo priest, he knew the advantages. Otherwise he couldn't get into that room.

The third man to walk in behind the monsignor and the police chief was Hank Herschel. An attorney representing the Toledo Diocese and, by extension, Father Robinson, he was a 1967 graduate of the University of Toledo Law School (who isn't in Toledo?).

"Bill," Vetter said to Kina, "would you step out of the room?"

Kina left. Vetter, Schmit, and Herschel met privately

behind closed doors with Father Robinson in the interview room. A short while later, the door opened. The detectives in the bureau watched as Toledo justice played out before them. Head held high, Father Gerald Robinson came out of the interview room.

"What are they doing?" Kina asked Swiatecki, who had also been watching.

"Well, they'll put him out on a funny farm, and you'll never hear from him again."

Escorted by the Debuty Chief Vetter, Monsignor Schmit, and attorney Herschel, Father Robinson was ushered out the front door of police headquarters.

Shortly afterward, the chief decided to break protocol. All police reports were normally filed in color-coded triplicate. The yellow copy went to the investigating office, the pink to the department for its files, and the white copy to the records section. On the Robinson case, Vetter made it protocol that *all* copies of police reports be given to him directly. That meant that except for what Vetter had, no other copies existed.

Or so he assumed.

This is the coat of arms of a monsignor
with the rank of Chaplain of His Holiness

Sometime after Robinson walked out of that interview room, or sauntered depending on who is telling the story, Edward Joshua Franks turned in the best piece of detective work on the case.

Within hours of being bagged, the letter opener found its way to the right guy, TPD criminalist Edward Joshua Franks. Franks found the four-sided blade to be pristine. There were no smears of any kind, including fingerprints, on blade or handle. It looked like somebody had taken great care in wiping them clean. Franks next turned to the wax medallion that showed the U.S. Capitol in relief. It would later be established that Father Robinson picked up the letter opener as a souvenir from a Washington, D.C., wax museum he had once visited. Franks decided to pry up the medallion and see if there was anything underneath.

A few weeks later, Franks had completed all his forensic tests and sent his report, dated April 25, 1980, to the detectives. The shoes turned up negative for blood. Robinson's contention that his cassock had gravy on it and not blood turned out to be correct. He also had a prescription from a medical doctor for the Valium. So far, there was nothing wrong. The letter opener was another matter. The forensics report on it stated the following:

Objective: To analyze for the possible presence of human blood.

Data: Analysis was performed by using bio-chemical techniques.

Conclusion: The wax medallion affixed to Exhibit 1 (letter opener) gave a weak positive result to a

presumptive screening test for blood, indicating the possible presence of blood.
Remarks: There was insufficient material present for the
conduct of confirmatory tests.

Using then current forensic technology, the criminalist couldn't say for sure there was blood under the medallion, just that it was highly possible. Still, as circumstantial evidence goes, it could be quite valuable in pointing an accusatory finger at the off-limits and protected Father Gerald Robinson. After all, the letter opener was his and had been in his possession at all times.

Vetter had Marx and Kina take their case to the Lucas County prosecutor, who was decidedly unimpressed with the evidence. The prosecutor claimed that since the lie test was inadmissible, and the results of the tests on the letter opener were inconclusive, it was too weak a case to take forward. In a crazy way, it made sense. The prosecutor was viewing the suspect not just as any suspect, but as a priest. The prosecutor knew that since Toledo was 25 percent Catholic, he could expect about three Catholics on any jury that tried Robinson. If any of them was so devout he refused to convict a priest for murder, that meant a hung jury every time.

As far as continuing to investigate Robinson, the TPD detectives had their proverbial hands tied behind their proverbial backs. If there's one good thing about the crime of murder, it's that a case stays open until it's closed. Unlike other crimes, there is no statute of limitation. Sure, the seventy-two-hour rule always applies—if you don't solve it in seventy-two hours when the clues are fresh, you may never solve it. Conducting a murder investigation when the prime suspect is off-limits is a particularly difficult job.

Essentially, Marx and Kina were in the position of laying off their prime suspect and instead following up every false lead that came their way as if there was something true about them. With the murder still unsolved, "leads" did pour into police headquarters, and the cops had to go through the motions of following up every one.

On March 22, 1981, less than a month before the one-year anniversary of the murder, Marx drove north to Ypsilanti State Hospital. Located in Ann Arbor, Michigan, Ypsilanti was the site of the Center for Forensic Psychiatry. Marx had an appointment with Dr. Harley Stock. Stock was a psychiatrist at the center who had offered the TPD a psychological profile of the hypothetical suspect involved in the Pahl homicide.

Dr. Harley Stock had quite a background. He was considered an expert authority in criminal profiling, hostage negotiation, and interview/interrogation methods. He had worked at the forensic center for the past four years and taught at the FBI Academy at Quantico, Virginia.

"Criminal profiling is not an exact science," Stock cautioned the detective. "That must be fully understood by those who intend to use the service."

That said, having viewed the case file and discussing all available information on the case, Stock was prepared to offer a profile of the hypothetical suspect responsible for the death of Sister Margaret Ann Pahl. Stock told Marx that the suspect was "a non-white male, mid-20's, possibly Spanish. He is extremely strong and he has a tenth to eleventh grade education."

Stock believed, "There is a history of family violence with the suspect possibly being the abused party. The suspect is heterosexual and he has very poor social relations, especially with women."

Gee, there's a surprise.

"The suspect is very repulsive, he can be violent and he is easily provoked. He does not [hold] himself responsible for his behavior. In this sense, he is mentally ill, but definitely not insane because he is sophisticated enough to blame others for his acts."

According to Stock, the original motive for Pahl's murder was robbery and not sexual assault or rape. After Marx asked him for some suggestions on how to approach and interview this type of suspect, Stock said it depends on the situation, as well as the conditions at the time of the interview. Stock felt that the interviewer should be "well rested, thus giving him a definite advantage."

"The best approach to interviewing the suspect," Stock added, "would include the concepts of time, space and the application of subtle pressure . . ."

Pressure was something the Toledo Diocese had used to protect one of its own to good effect. Sometime in 1981, Father Gerald Robinson, still the prime suspect in the Pahl homicide, packed his few bags containing his meager possessions—he had taken a vow of poverty as well as chastity to the Church—and said good-bye to Mercy Hospital for the last time. The Toledo Diocese had decided to transfer him to the Nativity, the Polish-speaking parish in another part of the city.

The idea was to bury him within the system of parishes run by the diocese, in exceedingly low-profile positions. No one within the diocese gave any indication that they feared a repeat incident. But this was not a case of priestly pedophilia, which would fill headlines in decades to come.

The Toledo Diocese had already reached out many times to the go-to boys in the TPD. Working together, the cops and the Church had already rescued pedophiliac priests from prosecution. But while pedophilia is a major felony and a tragedy for the victim and his family, it is nevertheless a felony that does not rise legally or morally to the level of murder. Murder is a whole other ball game, and that is what the Toledo Diocese did not count on.

Gerald Robinson was the prime suspect in a particularly heinous murder. If he killed once, what's to say he wouldn't kill again? No one knew for sure. They were just betting that if Robinson was innocent, they were doing the right thing, and if he was guilty, they were still doing the right thing because he was a priest. Regardless, the Toledo Diocese had gotten Robinson out of a pickle.

Watching over all this was the man at the top of the Toledo Diocese, Bishop John Anthony Donovan. A Canadian by birth, the sixty-nine-year-old priest had been created a bishop in 1954. Since 1967, he had served as the Toledo Diocese's fifth bishop. Donovan's titular headquarters was Our Lady of Most Holy Rosary Cathedral on Collingswood Boulevard.

Completed in 1931, Our Lady of Most Holy Rosary Cathedral is the central church of the diocese. According to the diocese's self history, "In 1979, Bishop John Donovan, our fifth shepherd, re-dedicated the altar (now brought forward to the people) amid a grateful throng who prayed, praised, and applauded with great gusto on the evening of September 18, opening a fresh chapter in diocesan history.

"As the mother church of the over 160 parishes of our diocese, Queen of the Most Holy Rosary leads the way as a twentieth century, renovated house of worship, while remaining an American-Medieval Cathedral of Spanish Plateresque style—an album of art; a sacred site; a story of faith in stone, paint, precious metal, glass, and wood."

Seven months later, Sister Margaret Ann Pahl was murdered, Father Gerald Robinson became the prime suspect, and Bishop John Anthony Donovan wasn't celebrating anymore. Nothing happened in Toledo without Bishop Donovan knowing about it, and nothing happened in the Church without him signing off on it. On July 29, 1980, Donovan did some signing of his own and suddenly resigned. In the history of the diocese from its inception in 1911 until 2007, Donovan is the only bishop to have resigned.

Perhaps he had a twinge of conscience. It is hard to tell, because Donovan died at age eighty on September 18, 1991, before anyone deposed him. No matter. With the clock forever stopped on the statute of limitations for murder, Sister Margaret Ann Pahl might still get justice.

PART TWO

PART TWO

CHAPTER 7

The Funny Farm

Growing up in postwar Toledo, the child of Polish parents, Jerry Robinson was raised multilingual in English and Polish in Kushwantz, one of Toledo's two Polish neighborhoods. He had a brother, John, who was eighteen years older.

As a child, Robinson attended Nativity Elementary, at the Polish-speaking Nativity church. His domineering mother was as proud as any devout Catholic would be when her teenage son Jerry chose the priesthood as his vocation. By the time Jerry Robinson came along, the machinery was already in place to help a young Polish boy like him to become a priest and serve the Polish Catholic community he grew up in and loved.

The SS. Cyril and Methodius Seminary was founded

in Detroit, Michigan, in 1885, eventually moving to the more rural Orchard Lake. The seminary's stated purpose was "to prepare candidates for the Roman Catholic priesthood primarily to serve Polish American immigrant communities." Its affiliated under-school was St. Mary's High School, also in Orchard Lake. Robinson attended St. Mary's in the early 1950s, a time of terrible political paranoia contrasted with *Father Knows Best, Ozzie and Harriet,* and other TV shows that extolled good, wholesome American values. People bought into this fantasy.

"I wish there was some way I could tell kids not to believe it—the dialogue, the situations, the characters—they were all totally false. The show did everybody a disservice," said Billy Gray, circa 1983, and quoted on IMDB.com. Gray played the character of Bud, the son on *Father Knows Best.*

"The girls were always trained to use their feminine wiles, to pretend to be helpless to attract men. The show contributed to a lot of the problems between men and women that we see today . . . I think we were all well motivated, but what we did was run a hoax. 'Father Knows Best' purported to be a reasonable facsimile of life. And the bad thing is that the model is so deceitful . . ." Gray continued.

Robinson, the high school projectionist, censored the films he showed during high school to his fellow seminarians, only picking the ones that were totally benign. People also bought the fantasy that priests were totally benign. In Kushwantz, they were sacrosanct.

As he studied for the priesthood at the SS. Cyril and Methodius Seminary, there was nothing about Robinson to distinguish him from his fellow seminarians, save, perhaps, for a cold, wintry manner and lack of emotion. The latter is consistently mentioned in printed accounts by those who knew him then, and just shrugged off as, "Oh, that's just Jerry."

All his friends noticed Jerry's "mild manner." He hated direct conflict; it made him ill. An emotional display just got to him. People said Jerry showed no emotion, that he was a quiet man, not in the John Wayne sense. Meek was more like it. Jerry Robinson showed all the classic attributes of *flat affect*. Something about his makeup made him unable to show emotions on his face, in his voice or manner. Everything was just flat-out the same in all those areas regardless of the circumstances.

When Sister Margaret Ann was murdered, it struck the detectives that Robinson showed a distinct lack of emotion regarding the crime. To them, that pointed at guilt, which of course made sense. If someone you worked with is suddenly murdered, you are supposed to show emotion of some sort: grief, anger, whatever. Never mind that shock can cause a seemingly emotionless reaction in the most emotional of persons. Cops think more in absolutes. Their job isn't to diagnose mental illness.

While some seminarians still dated women, having not yet taken their vows of chastity, Robinson never went out. It is quite possible that he never dated. That doesn't mean he never had sex. Many seminarians did. But Jerry Robinson had no intimate friends. He wasn't just a loner. There was something about him that made it seem he couldn't feel empathy.

It would be too easy, based just upon the observable details of his personality, to characterize Robinson as a sociopath. But if every sociopath in America committed murder, the police wouldn't have time to give out traffic tickets. Sociopaths, those who can't feel normal human emotion, especially empathy, are a lot more common in society than the average citizen realizes. Unfortunately, the word "sociopath" and its commonly used synonym "psychopath" are usually followed by the noun "murderer." That implies that one cannot exist without the other which is just plain bunk.

There are many individuals encountered in daily life who do not feel emotion as a normal human being might. We all know them—the boss who won't let up on us; the sadistic teacher; the storeowner who enjoys price gouging. These are people without consciences, sociopaths in everyday life. But for every one of them who winds up committing murder, the overwhelming majority live out their lives without anything more serious than a parking ticket. That's why the whole process of labeling criminals, especially by contemporary standards, can get dicey.

What gets even more confusing in the Pahl case is that once a man enters the Catholic priesthood, he literally disappears on record. The diocese itself maintains an internal personnel file on every priest. If a priest were reported to be a pedophile, for example, that report should theoretically repose in the priest's personnel file. If not, then it should be found in the diocesan secret files, which each diocese is obligated under Church edict to maintain. If it wasn't in either place, then it had to be in somebody's pocket file.

Before Jerry Robinson disappeared into the priesthood, a few things were evident. He had a domineering

mother who clearly influenced his choice of the priesthood as a vocation. He did not stand out in any way.
Superlatives were never attached to his name. He was
bound, as a century of Polish-speaking priests before
him, to serve out his time in Toledo's Polish-speaking
parishes.

Jerry Robinson was not especially charismatic, bound
for greatness, or any of that "great" stuff. He had shown
himself to be a controlling person in the way he censored
films he showed his peers. As for his sexuality, he appeared to have no interest in any sex. On May 30, 1964,
Gerald Robinson was ordained a Roman Catholic priest
at Queen of the Most Holy Rosary Cathedral in Toledo.
He got off to a resounding start at St. Adalbert's, where
he was hired as the fourth pastor out of four.

Despite his flat affect, Robinson still spoke Polish
and conducted services and confessions in the language.
That alone endeared him to his parishioners. Many
became lifelong supporters. The parish school's enroll-
ment was up to 771 children during Robinson's tenure
there, which lasted until 1973. Then the Toledo Diocese
offered him a step up the ladder, a promotion to associate pastor at Christ the King. Transferred there, he held
the post for three years and then inexplicably was transferred back to the dying St. Adalbert's.

For the good of his career, Robinson needed to get
out. He didn't have the luxury of "white flight" but he
did appear to have a guardian angel. The Toledo Diocese came through for him once again. The peripatetic
priest was transferred in 1974 to St. Michael's, where
he was, once again, associate pastor. Something had
to have happened at St. Michael's, though, because by

year's end, Robinson had already been transferred to the post of second listed chaplain at Mercy Hospital in 1974. He would eventually rise to first listed pastor.

At Mercy's chapel, Sister Margaret Ann Pahl's efficiency made it easy for him to perform the priestly rituals, from consecrating the host to giving the last rites. Bishop Donovan blessed the olive oil and made it holy every Thursday. Jerry Robinson, the extreme introvert, was forced to meet lots of people. Many of them were in dire emotional straits just by the nature of the chapel's location in a hospital.

After the murder, it was an entirely different matter. Like the Jews who had been cast out into the wilderness by God to pay for the sin of worshipping the Golden Calf, Jerry Robinson was cast out into the greater Toledo area by Bishop Donovan and the Toledo Diocese for the sin of being the prime suspect. For the Jews, their wandering in the Sinai Desert took forty years before God allowed them to enter the Promised Land. Jerry Robinson's time in purgatory would be closer to twenty-four years.

Robinson's first stop on the way to redemption was the Polish-speaking church of his youth, the Nativity. No more, however, was there a thriving children's school where congregants' kids were steeped in Polish Catholic culture. In fact, the school had long ceased to exist. Soon after Robinson's arrival in 1981, the church was shuttered for good in 1982. There Jerry Robinson was, a forty-four-year-old priest whom some people in Toledo were pretty certain had murdered a nun and gotten away with it. Now what? Once again, the diocese to the rescue. The diocese simultaneously assigned Robinson to two more of the dying Polish-speaking parishes, St. Stanislaus, where he was listed as "pastor," and St. Anthony's, where he was listed as "administrator."

"He and my dad became very good friends when Father was pastor of St. Stanislaus and Nativity," Barbara Ann Hall would later write. "I remember how happy my parents were when he brought a beautiful crucifix to them after Nativity closed. Since that time, the crucifix has a place of honor in our hallway. When you enter our home, your eyes go right to the crucifix."

Father Robinson was a special member of the Hall family.

"Speaking of generosity, he always gave Dad and me very generous gifts, always choosing *just the right gift*— Every Easter, a lily arrived. Every Christmas, a poinsetter [*sic*]. I know we were not the only recipients of his generosity," Hall continued. "He was very devoted to his mother taking her on trips, treating her like a queen. After her death, he visited the cemetery every day."

Robinson's travels took him in 1989 to the Toledo suburb of Sylvania. Talk about a low profile; he was the number three pastor out of three in Nowheresville, USA! He lasted there all of one year. But Father Gerald Robinson must have taken his time in the wilderness to reinvent himself. That is the only plausible explanation for what happened next.

Robinson had been serving out his time in the 1980s at parishes without schools. Though there is no criticism on record at the time that Robinson abused minors, the Church chose to post him at parishes where he had no contact with them. The Toledo Diocese eventually decided they could let him out on parole, to minister at churches with schools that held underage kids.

Father Gerald Robinson's wanderings were over. They had lasted a grand total of nine years. The state penalty for murder was considerably more than that—that is, if he was guilty. Regardless, the diocese moved Robinson up the ladder, making him in 1990 the second priest out of two serving the Polish-speaking parish faithful at St. Hedwig's. During his five years there, the parish school had 334 children listed in the church directory.

Elsewhere in Toledo, Marlo Damon lived with her mother, Doris; father, Robert; and older sisters, Ellen and Mara. Marlo was a dark-eyed brunette child who loved to write. She had a pet Labrador she called Smoky, played with dolls, and did all the normal things little girls do growing up. They lived in a small house, and spent summers in Shenandoah National Park. They fondly remembered the deer, which were as plentiful in the park's timberland as they were nonexistent in Toledo's urban jungle.

Unfortunately, Marlo had more than a little difficulty in her childhood. Like many millions of Americans, her mother, Doris, suffered from depression, which was serious enough to keep her homebound. Father Chet Warren used to stop by to counsel her. Father Warren, a tall, good-looking, broad-shouldered man, belonged to the priestly order of the Oblates of St. Francis de Sales.

Originally founded in the seventeenth century, the Oblates died out at the beginning of the eighteenth century. It would take another two hundred years before it was officially revived four days before Christmas in France, on December 21, 1875, by Pope Pius IX. In 1903 the Oblates control was decentralized and Westernized, with branches opened in England and the United States. It was in this order that Father Chet Warren served. Unfortunately, Warren had some problems too. It started with what he thought was his charm.

"After these counseling sessions with my mother," Marlo would later write, "he would encourage her to go upstairs and rest. When that happened, he'd watch me. On those occasions, he began sexually abusing me," Marlo would later write in a letter to the Toledo Diocese.

The abuse escalated, she later claimed in court documents.

"By the time I was in third grade, he [Father Warren] became physically violent as well. Sexual contact was becoming rougher and I would cry. Once he pulled my pigtails, slapped me across the face several times and told me this was just the beginning. Another time he sodomized me."

But that was nothing compared to the abuse she allegedly suffered at the hands of the cult. Marlo would later recall her father and grandfather being members of a satanic cult that included three Toledo priests, including Chet Warren. This cult met regularly, performing satanic rituals to honor their god, the fallen angel Satan. Marlo had been a part of many of them. Children were not only sexually molested during these ceremonies, they were ordered to observe as the adults abused other young victims.

One day when she was five, her father took her to Calvary Cemetery. There, the cult members were waiting. Marlo was put into a coffin and cockroaches put in to keep her company. Even for a healthy adult, such an experience would be mind-blowing, but for a child, it could have put Marlo into a catatonic state. Instead, her resiliency kept her going. After what had only been a few minutes but felt like forever, she was taken out of the box and the cockroaches crawled away.

That same year, Marlo's pet lab, Smoky, died. She loved Smoky. Like most kids, she was sad, but lo and behold! Marlo's dad woke her up a few nights later with the good news.

"Darling, we are going to see Smoky!"

That's what Marlo's father promised. The five-year-old got all excited at the prospect of seeing her beloved Smoky again. Like most kids, she had no understanding that death was final, and besides, she believed her dad.

"We arrived at an old house and down in the basement was a large table on which Smoky was laying. Dad and other adults changed into black robes." Marlo's sister grabbed a meat cleaver that someone gave her and proceeded to hack up Smoky. Arms and legs and head and blood seemed to be flying everywhere. When it was over, the cult had a message for Marlo.

"Chet told me that because I was such a bad girl [my sister] had to hurt Smoky like this. He then told me if I really loved Smoky, I would be able to put him back together and make him come back to life."

If Marlo was to be believed, a satanic cult including members of the Toledo's priesthood and other prominent Toledo citizens was operating within the Toledo Diocese. They appeared smart enough to use satanic mumbo-jumbo to instill guilt in an easily manipulated underage victim, the purpose being to avoid detection by the police. It is the kind of MO that so-called experts on satanic activity point to when saying there is an epidemic of this aberrant behavior.

Had the abuse stopped with dog mutilation, it never would have become relevant to the Pahl murder case, but it didn't. Five years later, things got worse.

"At age 11, they made me ingest an eyeball," she later told. "They wanted me to know they were always watching me."

Marlo claimed that her father had some sort of deal going with Warren. Her father would drop her off with Warren, who was working at St. Vincent's Hospital. The priest would then take her to his room, where he'd sell her sexual services to men who wanted a bit of sadomasochism with the Catholic school girl. It was in this context, of selling Marlo's sexual services, that the door to Warren's room allegedly opened.

In walked the grim figure of Father Gerald Robinson. Warren left them alone and closed the door. Like most childhood abuse victims, Marlo Damon said nothing to anyone. She felt ashamed, like it was her fault. She repressed the memories of what she claimed had been done to her by the cult and Father Robinson, forever, or so she thought.

The kind of behavior Marlo Damon describes is an almost textbook definition of ritual abuse.

Ritual abuse involves the sexual, physical, and psychological assault on a victim, by one or more "bad guys." The idea is to bring a ritual to fruition, thus satisfying the demands of the deity in question. It's important to understand that like most criminals, ritual abusers see nothing wrong with what they are doing. They are doing it to fill some inner, warped need. Since children are society's most defenseless individuals, ritual abusers target kids who can't fight back.

While popular literature suggests that some religious rituals involve sexual activity, the evidence trotted out to prove this is usually either anecdotal or fictional. However, historical literature suggests that an infamous Black Mass was conducted for the Marquise de Montespan, Louis XIV's mistress. The marquise's body served as the altar. The host was consecrated by sticking pieces into her vagina, and then they were consumed.

The idea of using the human body as an altar in a Black Mass was further described in detail in Anton Szandor LaVey's *Satanic Bible*, first published in 1969. While it is very rare for a child to be included in such sexual activity, it has happened and is documented. According to a major study into ritual abuse in Great Britain, three cases surfaced there where children were ritually abused as part of a satanic ceremony.

Considering his predilection for ceremony and ritual, it would not be hard to imagine a priest engaging in a satanic ceremony, especially during the time period in question when Satanism was a "hot" topic. The popularity of *The Exorcist, The Omen,* the Manson murder case in particular, LaVey's book, and other totems of popular culture had opened people's minds to the idea that Satanism actually existed in society and not just on screen or page.

Believing Robinson was a Satanist was difficult to swallow, but was it any more of a stretch than believing him to be a murderer? While he looked totally benign, Dave Davison had interviewed witnesses at the scene of the crime who all claimed the priest shook nuns when he got angry at them. If that was true, then the Church had early signs in the 1970s that Robinson had problems. Couple that with Damon's rape claim, and that made two major felonies Father Gerald Robinson was implicated in.

No matter. The Toledo Diocese had now put Father Gerald Robinson back on a career path suitable for a mid-life priest who still had a lot to give his parishioners.

CHAPTER 8

The Invisible Men

In 1996, the Toledo Diocese gave Jerry Robinson a promotion. Bishop James Hoffmann transferred him to the top spot at St. Vincent de Paul. Of course, Robinson was the only priest there. That still meant he was the big kahuna. But somewhat curiously, the church directory lists him as "administrator," rather than pastor.

The St. Vincent de Paul self history notes:

"In 1996, Fr. Thomas Gorman came to lead our flock. His sense of humor was wonderful and was a fine leader of our Parish. Fr. Gorman's stay was brief, however. Later that year, a kind, caring Pastor came to St. Vincent de Paul. He was Fr. Gerald Robinson."

What had happened was that St. John the Evangelist, another church in the parish, needed the dynamic Gorman's help. The parish was facing a contentious church renovation project. Having served there before, beginning in 1959, "I remembered the people from then as good people who I got along with well. I had good memories of my time here in the 1960s," Gorman later told a reporter.

That left a vacancy back at St. Vincent de Paul. Into the breach came Father Gerald Robinson.

"His gentle hand led us in worship for about nine months. In that time he made many friends in the parish. But, unfortunately, his stay at St. Vincent de Paul was brief . . ."

Robinson served only nine months at the church. Even for him that was a brief time. Interestingly enough, when Robinson left St. Vincent de Paul, something strange happened. The church's Web site just notes the superficial details:

"We had the honor to have Bishop James Hoffman come to lead us in worship. He wanted to take an active role in the Central Cities Ministries of Toledo, which St. Vincent de Paul is a part of. Since he spent some time at our Parish, he figured we were his best choice. He fit in very well with us and it seemed he never left. He remembered a lot of our parishioners from when he was with us in the 1970's. He then took a role in getting us our current Pastor."

What was not addressed in the church's public history was the strangeness of it all. Not only did Robinson have a brief tenure at St. Vincent de Paul's, a bishop—not another priest, not a member of the monsignori, the bishop himself! of the 300,000-plus member diocese—took the place of a lowly priest who was a whisper away from being indicted for murder.

As if the case were not weird enough, the diocese decided to take a page out of H. G. Wells.

"You don't understand," he said, "who I am or what I am. I'll show you. By Heaven! I'll show you." That is what Wells wrote in his 1897 novel *The Invisible Man*. That stranger, it turns out, is Griffin, a chemist who tinkered with the unnatural at peril to his humanity. He does indeed get his life's desire to become invisible, but the trade-off is that the invisibility formula he invented slowly turns him into a psychotic murderer. The Invisible Man had the hubris to think that because he was invisible, he was all-powerful, only to find he had the same weakness as all mortal men.

"Then came a mighty effort, and the Invisible Man threw off a couple of his antagonists and rose to his knees. Kemp clung to him in front like a hound to a stag, and a dozen hands gripped, clutched, and tore at the Unseen. The tram conductor suddenly got the neck and shoulders and lugged him back.

"Down went the heap of struggling men again and rolled over. There was, I am afraid, some savage kicking. Then suddenly a wild scream of 'Mercy! Mercy' that died down swiftly to a sound like choking."

Gerald Robinson had certainly not been proven a psychotic murderer, or anything close to it. The diocese he served, however, chose to treat him like Griffin after his brief stay at St. Vincent de Paul's. From 1997 on, Robinson's activities within the Church begin to get murky. There are inconsistencies in the Church's own record over where Robinson was and what he was doing.

By the millennium, Robinson had been taken off the official rolls. He was not listed or indexed in the *Official Catholic Directory, 2000–2005*. It was as neat a disappearing act as anything Griffin had done through his diaspora over the English countryside. Here in Toledo, the diocese had done well. The only times Robinson surfaced in an official capacity during this period were special guest appearances at St. Hyacinth's, another of Toledo's Polish-speaking parishes. Every Sunday during Lent, Robinson celebrated the Polish Lamentation of Our Lord's Passion at St. Hyacinth's.

In most "cold" cases like the Pahl homicide, after a certain passage of years, witnesses begin to die, not the least of which are the suspects. In the Pahl murder, there was only one, Robinson. Despite those mysterious accounts of a strange Chicano/African American hanging out around the chapel at the time of the murder, none of those racist "leads" had ever panned out.

By all accounts, Father Robinson was an alcoholic, though no one ever saw him drunk in public, which meant he imbibed in private. That doesn't mean he wasn't loaded when he was in public. Many alcoholics function quite well when they have a high blood alcohol level. Unlike most people, their tolerance for alcohol is enormous.

Comparing photographs of Jerry Robinson from 1964, 1980, and 2004, the difference is startling. He goes from a robust-looking man in 1964 and 1980 to a sagging old man in record time. Alcohol breaks down tissue elasticity. There are signs that alcohol, and potentially murder, took an incredible toll on him. His face looks like it melted. If that were any indication of what his liver was like, the prime suspect in Margaret Ann Pahl's murder had a pretty good shot, no pun intended, of avoiding prosecution by simply dying.

Considering the effort that had gone into making certain Robinson avoided prosecution, a lot of people in Toledo were hoping that would happen. Forget about a cold case; they wanted this one in the deep freeze. The problem was Dave Davison wouldn't look the other way.

Davison felt terrible when he first saw Sister Margaret Ann Pahl on the terrazzo floor of the sacristy. Perhaps he identified too much. He felt that it could just as easily have been his grandmother.

He knew what had happened in the Pahl case. He knew the department had dropped it deliberately. Any cop with half a brain knew that. How else to explain a "hands off" on the prime suspect? Davison went about his business, determined not to drop the case, regardless of what the department said.

In 1988, Davison had worked his way up to acting sergeant. On a cold December 16, he stopped a kidnapping in progress without even getting out of his police car. Despite the cold, he had been driving around with the window down so he could hear if there was trouble.

"If you keep the window up and the heater on you cannot monitor the outside effectively. Plus you have the radio traffic," Davison continues.

Suddenly, a car rammed into him.

"When the lady made the correct decision to hit me she did the smart thing and gunned her engine. Because I had the window down I heard that engine pitch so I leaned forward so I could look behind me. That is how most of my injuries happened."

Moments before, inside that vehicle, thirty-two-year-old Selma Blair; her two sons, Abel, age eleven months, and Stuart, age three years; plus Mrs. Blair's sixty-year-old mother, June Clayton, had been kidnapped by a knife-wielding assailant. The kidnapper held his knife to the throat of eleven-month-old Abel, and Blair was forced to get behind the wheel. Then she did something few mothers or fathers would have the courage to do. Knowing they had a better chance of dying if they kept going with the knife-wielding "bad guy," she rammed into Davison's police car, which was stopped at a light, to break up the kidnapping in progress.

"Since my shoulder harness was stretched by my pulling forward to turn so I could look behind me, when she hit me I was pulled backwards hard. My head struck the headrest and I really did see bright flashes of light for a few seconds."

Davison eventually reached for his radio and called for a life squad.

"The harness dug into my chest so hard I honestly

thought I was having a heart attack. The wind had been knocked out of me. The lady who hit me ran up to my vehicle and opened my door."

"Aren't you going to chase that man?" said Blair.

"I undid my harness and fell out of the car and into the street. I remember there was a lot of snow and slush. I could not stand up at that point. I asked the lady to describe the man and to tell which way he had run. I put that information out over the radio and told the dispatcher to send the crews that were coming to go after the suspect. I also asked him to cancel the life squad because by this time I knew I was not having a heart attack."

Cops caught the kidnapper a few blocks away. By that time, the intersection was swimming with cops and ambulance crews. "By that time I was able to stand. I told the fire and rescue crews that I was fine so they left. Police crews kept coming over to me and saying that the dispatcher was calling me but I never heard him. I got into my vehicle and drove myself to the hospital.

"At the hospital I kept repeating, 'A lady hit me with her car.' The other people in the waiting room moved away from me quickly."

After Davison kept repeating himself, someone finally figured out that he had a big-time concussion.

"While they were treating me on a gurney, a command officer walked into the room and told me that the amount of damage to me showed that I could not have been wearing my shoulder harness so all the injuries were my own fault. At that point, the doctor who was standing there lifted up my shirt and showed him the mark across my chest where the harness had dug in. The command officer stormed out of the room without another word."

His luck holding true, Dave Davison really became the accident's only physical victim. Holding true to form, the TPD "Unusual Incident Report" contains more information on the condition of the damaged police car than Davison's body. The injuries included broken vertebrae, partial hearing loss, and severe concussion. But the TPD in its infinite wisdom didn't believe him.

"They regularly sent a command officer out to my house to make sure I was at home and not running around. The command officer would knock on my door with his nightstick, ring the bell, and yell my name until I got out of bed and made it to the door. This kept up until I tried to go back.

"The concussion kicked my ass for the holidays. I had little short term memory. I made out my Christmas cards and I went to put my coat on so I could mail them out. By the time I put my coat on and picked up my car keys I had no idea why I was dressed and ready to go somewhere. Just by chance I walked past the cards on the kitchen table.

"I interviewed for the position of full time sergeant while I was still fuzzy. They turned me down for the job because I kept looking out a window at a pigeon on a wire while they questioned me about why I should be a command officer. I think that pigeon saved me from crossing over to the dark side because they turned my promotion down.

"That's how I got my disability," Davison explains. "The injuries got worse over the year and by 1990, I retired on disability."

Davison lived in a suburban though still rundown Toledo neighborhood of identical small, whitewashed ranch homes. Dave Davison was looking at his new business card. It was totally unique and with his dry sense of humor totally described his predicament: "Retired."

For fifteen years, Davison had been obsessed with a murder case that no one wanted solved, least of all the Toledo Diocese, the Toledo Police Department, and the Lucas County Prosecutor's Office. Now he was determined to find out the truth about Robinson. He decided to run a con.

"My idea," Davison says softly, "was to panic them into movement. If they thought I was writing a book, they couldn't sit on my request. They would think I had a publisher behind me."

Claiming he was authoring a book about the murder of Sister Margaret Ann Pahl, Davison filed a Freedom of Information Request with the TPD for copies of the records of her murder investigation. While waiting for a response, Davison picked up quill again, this time asking the U.S. Department of Justice for assistance.

Their response:

There was no way the feds could intervene in a local case, no matter what kind of corruption, unless there was a violation of federal law. If, for example, the TPD had used the U.S. mails to cover up the murder, then the feds could move in and investigate. But without that kind of egregious violation of federal law, the feds had to stay out of a local community's business.

U. S. Department of Justice

Criminal Division

_____

Washington, D.C. 20530

February 10, 1995

Mr. Dave D. Davison

Dear Mr. Davison:

Thank you for your letter to the Attorney General. She has asked me to respond to you on her behalf regarding your concern about local law enforcement. Please understand that the Department of Justice can assume jurisdiction only when there has been a possible violation of the federal criminal statutes. From the information you provided, we are unable to ascertain whether any violations of this nature have occurred. If you have reason to believe there has been a violation of the federal criminal statutes, and you have further, more specific evidence, you should contact the local office of the Federal Bureau of Investigation (FBI), which is the investigatory arm of the Department of Justice. If the facts warrant, it will conduct an investigation and present the results to the appropriate United States Attorney's office for a prosecutorial evaluation; and, in the event any inquiry conducted by the FBI uncovers evidence of a violation of federal criminal law, the Department of Justice would be advised.

Additionally, the Department of Justice, the federal agency which is most closely involved with the criminal justice system, has no supervisory authority over local law enforcement. Even if local law enforcement authorities do not perform as well as you believe they should, in the absence of a violation of federal law, the Executive Branch of the federal government has no authority to intervene. I suggest that you make your complaints known to the mayor or members of your city council and, perhaps, the state's prosecuting attorney, as well.

The Attorney General appreciates the confidence which prompted you to write her.

Sincerely,

Pamela A Spraker

Pamela A. Spraker
Executive Office

FST002A   1A32152

Meanwhile, the TPD had responded to his request for records to write a "book":

CITY OF **TOLEDO** OHIO

DEPARTMENT OF POLICE OPERATIONS
SAFETY BUILDING

Carleton S. Finkbeiner
Mayor

525 N. Erie Street
Toledo, Ohio 43624-1345

Chief Gerald T. Galvin
Director of Police Operations
(419)245-3200
(Fax)245-3228

March 17, 1995

Dave D. Davison

███████████████████

Re: Public Records Request

Dear Mr. Davison:

With reference to your request for "records and files" related to the murder of Sister Margaret Ann Pahl in the spring of 1980, please be advised that Sergeant Marx has never been assigned as the person responsible to provide these documents.

A records search has revealed that the Toledo Police Department is in possession of a number of reports connected with the incident you described. Since this case has never been solved, however, much of the information contained within these reports is regarded as confidential and is protected by law. Therefore, although you may be provided with copies of virtually all of the reports, much of the information may be redacted or deleted.

If you desire copies of these reports, you may submit a written request to: Public Records, Toledo Police Department Records Section, 525 N. Erie Street, Toledo, Ohio 43624. A nominal charge of $ .20 will be made for each page provided.

Sincerely,

Michael Navarre.

Michael Navarre
Deputy Chief
Centralized Services

MN:mm

< To Protect and Serve >

Holy shit, it worked, Davison thought. *They don't even know who I am!* Anxiously, he sat down to write his next letter:

```
Public Records
Toledo Police Department
Records Section
525 N. Erie Street
Toledo, Ohio 43624
```

Dear Ms. Mohr:

If possible I would like to have copies of any and all reports and files related to the murder of Sister Margaret Ann Pahl in the spring of 1980. I have been in contact with Deputy Chief Michael Navarre and he advised me to make a written request to you. I fully understand that much of the information in the reports will be redacted or deleted. I am working on a book dealing with Sister Pahl and her murder so even what is not included or is blacked out will serve a purpose.

If you will be kind enough to give me a phone call to let me know how much I owe for the work and your time I will bring a check or cash with me when I pick up the materials. I thank you in advance for both your time and effeort. Also, I don't know if you remember me, but if you do...Hello Helen. Thanks again.

                    Sincerely,

                    Dave D. Davison

                    ███████████████████████

  While waiting for a response, Davison next wrote to Ohio governor George Voinovich about the case and the way the TPD had handled it. The governor's response?

GEORGE V. VOINOVICH
GOVERNOR

STATE OF OHIO
OFFICE OF THE GOVERNOR
COLUMBUS 43266-0601

March 14, 1995

Mr. Dave D. Davison

████████████████████

Dear Mr. Davison:

This is to acknowledge receipt of your letter to Governor Voinovich. The Governor has asked me, as his liaison on criminal matters, to respond.

Please be advised the Governor has no legal authority to intervene in municipal police investigations. I would suggest you contact the city or county prosecutor in Toledo with your concerns.

Thank you for your letter, I hope you find this information helpful.

Sincerely,

Karen J. Huey

Karen J. Huey
Assistant Deputy Legal Counsel

kjh/kh

Voinovich was the governor. He could certainly ask the state prosecutor, the Ohio state attorney general, to look into the matter and report back to him. Instead, Davison got a brush-off letter that defied common sense. Next, Davison wrote the bishop of the Toledo Diocese who had replaced Donovan, James R. Hoffman. He asked Hoffman for assistance in investigating Sister Margaret Ann Pahl's unsolved murder. The bishop responded personally:

DIOCESE OF TOLEDO
Office of the Bishop
1933 Spielbusch Ave.
Toledo, OH 43624

Mailing Address:
Box 985
Toledo, OH 43697-0985

Phone
419-244-6711

June 2, 1995

Mr. Dave D. Davison
████████████████████

Dear Mr. Davison:

With this letter, I wish to acknowledge your correspondence of May 1995.

As to your request, I would offer this response.

The homicide to which you refer took place on April 5, 1980. At that time my predecessor, John A. Donovan, was the Bishop of the Diocese of Toledo. I was serving as the pastor of St. Joseph Parish, Sylvania. I was not privy to the details of any contact that may have taken place between police investigators and Bishop Donovan.

I do remember hearing that detectives had spoken to several priests who were chaplains at Mercy Hospital, Toledo. I was of the impression that the priest/chaplains had given full cooperation with the authorities.

I know of nothing that would be helpful to your inquiry.

Sincerely yours,

James R. Hoffman
Bishop of Toledo

JRH:mlh

Under Vatican edict, every diocese maintains a secret archive that contains top-secret information on all priestly activity within the diocese. Hoffman knew this, though no one else outside the church did at the time. Hoffman could have opened those records to Davison. It was an unsolved homicide of a nun within Hoffman's diocese. Instead, Hoffman chose to ignore Davison's request. Less than two years later, Bishop Hoffman would relieve Father Robinson of his duties at St. Vincent de Paul.

Davison had the patience of a saint. If he hadn't been imitating Don Quixote tilting at windmills before, he certainly did with his next letter. He sent it to the Pope John Paul II, care of the Vatican, informing him of the unsolved 1980 murder of a sister of the Roman Catholic Church in Toledo—the Pope was Polish and sure to know the parish's history—and the fact, *the fact*, that *a priest* of that same church had been the prime suspect in the unsolved homicide.

The response came swiftly:

SECRETARIAT OF STATE
———
FIRST SECTION · GENERAL AFFAIRS

From the Vatican, July 25, 199

Dear Mr. Davison,

I am directed to acknowledge your most recent letter to His Holiness Pope John Paul II, and I would assure you that the contents have been carefully noted.

With good wishes, I remain

Sincerely yours,

Sandri

Monsignor L. Sandri
Assessor

Mr. David D. Davison

While the letter appeared to be another brush-off, it had found its way to the right party.

Another distinguished member of the monsignori, L. Sandri was a church assessor. According to the *Catholic Encyclopedia*, the title of assessor has a twofold meaning. The assessor can be a judge in a collegiate tribunal or one who assists the presiding judge in interpreting the law. "In the latter meaning assessors are simply advisers of the judge, who aid him to obtain a full knowledge of the case and by their advice, helping him to decide justly."

Assessor Sandri's interpretation seemed to be that no further Vatican action was warranted in the case. The Vatican never contacted Davison again. Pope John Paul II probably never knew of the charges in the one diocese in the United States where he surely had to feel at home. It would be hard to believe that the pope of the Roman Catholic Church would ever be content to let the murder of one of the church's most devoted servants, a nun, go unsolved simply because a priest was implicated.

Then the phone rang. Davison picked it up.

"Hello, this is Sonja McMahon down in records. I have your FOIA request and I've got three hundred pages of documents for you. When can you come pick it up, and bring your checkbook?"

Davison couldn't believe it! Had his bluff actually worked?

"I had a friend who did the FOIA requests," Davison says. "To this day, I think she did me a favor."

He ran down to the second floor of the Records Bureau downtown. There was a bounce to his step that hadn't been there for fifteen years. In the corner closest to the municipal court across the street was a large office. Davison opened the door into a huge room, where about twenty people sat at desks. They were the custodians of the records of the TPD.

"This lady brought the stuff up to me. It was flapping loose," Davison says. "I took it home and went through it, outlining in colored marker the sections I thought were most relevant to the case."

Ray Vetter's hubris perhaps made him think that he had gotten all the copies of the reports on the Pahl homicide. He hadn't. Someone had held out. The three hundred pages of police reports covered much of the initial investigation. But every mention of Robinson as the prime suspect was either blacked out or purged completely. That included Davison's own supplemental reports with the people on the scene who implicated Robinson as the prime suspect.

Some of the censoring had been done very poorly by someone who wasn't very bright. Many pages contained enough detailed descriptions of persons and events to make them clearly identifiable, no matter that names were blacked out. Taken all together, the reports showed a textbook homicide investigation cut short at the point that Robinson became the prime suspect.

The papers were notable for what they didn't contain: the results of the autopsy of Margaret Ann Pahl. Davison made another FOIA request for the autopsy report. But it was too late.

"They figured out what was happening. They lied to me," Davison claimed. "The records people told me that the case had been reactivated. They said that the case had been given to Lieutenant Gary Lockwood, who was currently investigating. I didn't get anything else."

According to Davison, Lucas County prosecutor Anthony Pizza found out what had happened. Buying the "con" that Davison was writing a true crime book, he told the retired cop that he better prove his charges of a police cover-up in his book or they'd sue him and own him. Davison didn't mind. There wasn't much he owned but his neat little house. Inside of course was a different matter.

Dave Davison is an animal nut. He has four dogs rescued from the Toledo Humane Society; six birds, most of which he got from people who died and the animals had nowhere to go; two turtles and four frogs, all found in his yard over the years; one very large spider from Mexico; and finally five lizards, most of which were given to him when their owners got tired of them.

"In truth I cut myself off from people because I came to the conclusion I preferred animals to people," he says.

It's a good thing he has a cop's pension, otherwise his animals would starve. Now, if they went after his animals, *that* would be a different story.

For now, Dave Davison was content to hoard the documents. He had tried as hard as he could to get someone outside Toledo interested enough in the case that they would push it through to its conclusion. That had not happened. Davison was realistic enough to know that while things weren't working to his benefit now, that didn't mean in five or ten years, there might not be an opportunity to prosecute the son-of-a-bitch.

Dave Davison settled down to wait. As long as it took, he was intent on getting "Father Jerry" for murder.

CHAPTER 9

The Satanists

Suddenly, it was June 1692 in damp Salem, Massachusetts. Innocent people were being accused of satanic abuse. Only it wasn't. It was August 1983 in beautiful, sunny Southern California.

In the Los Angeles suburb by the sea, Manhattan Beach, seventy-nine-year-old Virginia McMartin, fifty-nine-year-old Peggy Buckey, and her twenty-eight-year-old son Ray Buckey were accused by the mother of one of their preschoolers of sexually abusing and torturing children in satanic rites at their Manhattan Beach day care center. It was about as bizarre a story as any to come down the crime pike.

The prosecutor, the L.A. District Attorney's Office, relentlessly pursued the accused. The case snowballed as outside "experts" counseled most of the children at the day care center into believing they had all been victimized. That led to the DA charging the defendants and bringing them to trial twice in 1989 and 1990, for sexually abusing the children under their care. Both of the trials ended in hung juries. After the second trial, Los Angeles DA Ira Reiner wisely dropped all charges.

The McMartin Preschool abuse trials turned out to be the longest and most expensive criminal trials in American history. Fueled by the baseless charges of a woman who it turned out had emotional problems, the elected representative of the citizens of Los Angeles County had spent seven years of taxpayers' time and $15 million of their money investigating and prosecuting a case without any convictions. When it was all over, the victims were two-fold: the kids who had implanted memories of satanic sexual abuse by the so-called experts, and the defendants whose lives and careers were ruined by the baseless charges. Ray Buckey spent five years in jail without bail, waiting for the trial.

But people in California and the rest of the country were only too ready to believe the satanic charges they heard during the McMartin Preschool trials. The media diligently complied, following every turn of the trials and sensationalizing them whenever they could, which only served to obscure the truth—a national epidemic of satanic abuse cases began to be reported. From coast to coast, stories emerged of children being beaten, sexually abused, tortured, and in some instances, used as human sacrifices by satanic cults.

Hard evidence being at a premium, most if not all of

these cases would eventually prove to be specious. That made no difference. A conservative social climate swept through the United States in the 1980s, where people were wont to believe the worst in their neighbors. The same thing had happened in Salem, Massachusetts, in 1692.

The Salem witch hunt murders started when a West Indian slave called Tituba performed magic tricks for the daughters of Samuel Parris, pastor of Salem Village. Eventually, the circle for which she performed widened to include other curious friends. But Tituba's magic had the curious effect of making some of the girls act irrationally.

A local doctor was called to treat the young women. A doctor in 1692 really was worse than no doctor at all. Dr. Staunch Protestant White Guy pronounced the girls bewitched. That made it a clerical matter. The girls were intensely questioned by the town's clerics. When asked who had bewitched them, they accused Tituba "and two derelict women in the community."

That made sense: accuse the disenfranchised rather than the privileged. All three were arrested. Some sort of archaic good cop/bad cop questioning followed during which Tituba, seeing the proverbial handwriting on the wall, informed on the other two. She got off. The other two hanged.

They had been condemned by a hastily put together court of attainder that had no legal authority. Despite that, from then on, anyone could be accused of being a witch in Salem and executed. When it was finally over, a total of twenty people lost their lives as a result of the state-sponsored Salem witch trials.

In 1985, the satanic cult hysteria that had swept the country found its way into Toledo, that backward pocket of civilization on Lake Erie. A Toledo resident told the police that he had been a member of a satanic cult operating in the greater Toledo area. The cult was responsible for the deaths of sixty to seventy-five infants, children, and adults. The charges sounded outrageous but Deputy Sheriff James Telb, Lucas County Sheriff's Department, took them seriously.

As anyone of a later generation who has watched *The Sopranos* knows, getting rid of a dead body is not an easy thing. It's the same in reality. Where do you put so many bodies? Do you dig graves? Ever try to dig seventy-five graves deep enough so the bodies aren't discovered? Seventy-five holes, even smaller ones for the kids, would be impossible to keep secret.

Or maybe you decide to cut them up. Ever try cutting up seventy-five bodies? Lot of blood. That's a lot of evidence. Luminol can illuminate the most microscopic traces of blood. Distributing body parts from seventy-five bodies is also not an easy thing. Then again, how about burning the bodies during a satanic rite? One problem: you could never get the fire hot enough outdoors or indoors to completely burn the bodies. Unless you used a professional crematorium, bones and other organic matter would be left for identification.

Telb followed up the complaint by leading a dig at three sites in Spencer Township, a Toledo suburb west of the city. Quickly, the three sites of alleged satanic sacrifice were excavated in twenty-four hours. Deputy Sheriff Telb told the *Chronicle-Telegram* newspaper,

"Artifacts [discovered] included two large knives, a doll with its feet nailed to a board and a pentagram medal tied to its wrist, wooden crosses, and red twine wound through bushes and grass around the three excavation sites."

A reporter for the *Columbus Post Dispatch* dryly observed, "Hanging from a tree branch next to a rural Lucas County road was what for all the world appeared to be a piece of red string, perhaps six inches long. It wasn't knotted or arranged in any way. It just hung there about eye level, waiting for the wind to carry it to the ground or for an expert on Satanism to call it a tool of devil worship and possible evidence of ritual murders."

Deputy Sheriff Telb insistently told the same newspaper on June 22, 1985, "We know there's a cult here. There's no question there's a cult operating in Lucas County. We found enough evidence here to substantiate that."

If they did, nothing ever came of it. The national media that had converged on Toledo to cover the "Lucas County incident," slowly dispersed to tackle the next story of national insignificance. Then TV took it a step further. People labeling themselves as "Survivors of Satanic Cults!" appeared on trashy daytime talk shows. The ratings on these freak shows soared through the late 1980s and into the middle 1990s.

By 1995 the truth was starting to be known. A national scandal had erupted in the therapeutic community. So-called therapists, many with nothing more than a one-year master's in social work, had implanted memories in their patients' psyches. They had encouraged them to believe they had been satanically abused when they had not. Lawsuits and settlements followed. Then, with the dawn of the millennium, reports of satanic cults died away, to be replaced by reports of priests sexually abusing minors in their care.

Beginning in 2001, priestly sexual abuse scandals rocked the Catholic Church. This time, there was hard evidence that could not be refuted. After decades of covering up for pedophiliac priests, the Church had finally wised up long after rank-and-file Catholics did. Even the most devout Catholics had long ago discovered that the saintly and chaste Father O'Malley and the grouchy and chaste Father Fitzgibbon were Hollywood creations. Across the United States in parish after parish, priests were accused of sexually abusing minors in their care.

The first clerical sexual abuse scandal to hit Toledo during this period involved the Oblates priest, Father Chet Warren. Back in 1993 eight women had come forward with credible evidence of clerical abuse by Father Warren. The Toledo Diocese realized the charges were probably true. They did what parishes around the country had started to do in similar circumstances: they made a deal for the priest to quietly leave the priesthood. Warren was defrocked.

One of Warren's alleged childhood victims, Teresa Bombrys, had moved to Columbus. In 2002, forty-four-year-old Brombrys sued Warren, the Oblates, and the Toledo Diocese for damages relating to her alleged abuse at Warren's hands and other parts of his body. The story was covered in the *Toledo Blade,* where a now adult Marlo Damon read it. Damon started to sweat and have flashbacks to her abuse. She knew Chet Warren intimately.

Marlo Damon had never voiced her claims of childhood satanic abuse by her father and his cult of Satan worshippers, including Warren and the Catholic priests of the Toledo Diocese. Despite her trauma, she had grown up to become an important member of society—a nun. Though she didn't know it, Sister Marlo Damon and Sister Margaret Ann Pahl had much in common. In some strange way, they were connected though they never met and were certainly not related. When they did eventually come together, some would look at one as being the savior of the other.

Damon served her Lord as one of the Sisters of the Cathedral, an order founded by Emelie Starker in Hungary, 1894. Since then the order has grown to a thirty-two-hundred-member international congregation on four continents, divided into geographic units called segments. With the mother house based in Rome, there are five segments in the United States including Toledo, where the sisters have been ministering to the poor since 1899.

As a devout Catholic, becoming a nun was a way for Damon to fight back against her childhood abuse. In some ways, it might have been her only choice. *Catechism of the Catholic Church, Second Edition,* Section II, The Fall of the Angels, speaks eloquently of who is the real enemy of Catholics.

"Behind the disobedient choice of our first parents lurks a seductive voice, opposed to God, which makes them fall into death out of envy. Scripture and the Church's Tradition see in this being a fallen angel, called

'Satan' or the 'devil.' The Church teaches that Satan was at first a good angel, made by God: 'The devil and the other demons were indeed created naturally good by God, but they became evil by their own doing.'"

In choosing to serve her Lord, Jesus Christ, Damon was choosing to fight the one Jesus called "'a murderer from the beginning,' who would even try to divert Jesus from the mission received from his Father. 'The reason the Son of God appeared was to destroy the works of the devil.'"

Satan was behind her abuse. Satan needed to be fought, and defeated.

"It is a great mystery that providence should permit diabolical activity, but 'we know that in everything God works for good with those who love him.'"

In 2002, Sister Marlo Damon wasn't questioning God. Not at all. What she was questioning was why she had to keep shelling out for expensive psychotherapy. It really didn't make much sense. Shouldn't those ultimately responsible for the actions of the priests who she says abused her be the ones who paid? With all the attention the public and media had given the cases of priestly pedophilia, wasn't it right that the same attention be paid to the satanic abuse she had described? It was a perfectly logical argument.

While Sister Marlo Damon was going through this self-questioning process, she had flashbacks to her satanic abuse sessions. Simultaneously, the Church was having its own problems with flashbacks. The Vatican finally figured out that whatever policy they had in place to take care of clerical abuse just wasn't cutting it. They needed to deal with the problem or face further defections from the ranks of practicing Catholics.

In 2002, the U.S. Conference of Catholic Bishops held a convocation in Dallas, Texas. The document all the bishops agreed to came to be known as the Dallas Charter. The church refers to it formally as the *Charter for the Protection of Children and Young People*. Primarily, it is a mea culpa for all the cases of priestly abuse.

"The Church in the United States is experiencing a crisis without precedent in our times. The sexual abuse of children and young people by some priests and bishops and the ways in which bishops have addressed these crimes and sins, have caused enormous pain, anger and confusion. Innocent victims and their families have suffered terribly."

Then came the confession.

"In the past," the charter preamble continued, "secrecy has created an atmosphere that has inhibited the healing process and in some cases enabled sexually abusive behavior to be repeated. As bishops we acknowledge our mistakes and our role in that suffering, and we apologize and take responsibility for too often failing victims and our people in the past. We also take responsibility in dealing with this problem strongly, consistently, and effectively in the future. From the depths of our hearts we bishops express great sorrow and profound regret for what the Catholic people are enduring."

It was an astonishing document and if carried through to its logical conclusion, could revolutionize the way the church dealt with clerical abuse cases. Most importantly, to advance the promises to protect children, dioceses in every state would set up internal review boards to hear victims' allegations and make recommendations on how to proceed.

Sister Marlo Damon took the charter seriously. Being a good nun, she believed in the system in which she served, that she could get justice from it without going to an outside body. Therapy had given her value as a person. That's why she was angry.

Why should she have to continue paying for what those people had done to her? She had no money; she had taken a vow of poverty. Like all nuns, she was given only a pittance to live on. It was out of those meager funds that she saved for her therapy. Her order had helped with her bills, but they were tapped out. The financial burden was crushing.

Sister Marlo Damon believed in her Church, she believed in the Dallas Charter, she believed in her order, and she believed in the Toledo Diocese. After all, Sister Marlo Damon reasoned, she had God on her side. He was with her when she picked up the phone and called Frank DiLallo. Frank DiLallo was the diocese's case manager. Damon asked for a meeting, to which DiLallo agreed.

At their meeting, Sister Marlo Damon quickly got to the point—she wanted the Toledo Diocese to pay fifty grand to cover her present and future counseling and medication expenses. Challenged to explain why the diocese should foot the bill, Damon told him that she had been raped by Father Chet Warren.

DiLallo reminded Damon that Warren had been an Oblates priest, outside the jurisdiction of the Toledo

Diocese. Anyway, he'd been kicked out of the priesthood. Damon wasn't a nun for nothing. She reminded *him* that any priest serving in the diocese did so at the pleasure of the bishop, putting said priest under the diocese's jurisdiction.

DiLallo wisely deferred the matter until he could investigate further. It was, after all, an unusual situation. He promised to get back to her. Four months later, Damon once again called DiLallo. What was happening about her complaint? She wanted a second meeting. DiLallo agreed. He didn't know that Damon, though she might have been naïve, wasn't about to let the diocese slide on its responsibility.

At the second meeting, Damon came with compelling documentation. There was a copy of a letter from her mother superior demanding that the diocese grant Sister Marlo's payment as requested—$50K. Also, she had a pharmacist's statement regarding her considerable cost for medication.

As 2003 progressed, Damon and her attorney—she had smartened up and got one—pressed their case. Damon contacted Claudia Vercellotti, passionate victims rights advocate for SNAP (Survival Network of Those Abused By Priests), and told Vercellotti of her claim. Vercellotti began advising her. One year almost to the day that the Dallas Charter was passed, Sister Marlo Damon was invited to testify before the Toledo Diocesan Review Board. The latter consisted of the only non-Catholic, psychologist Dr. Robert Poole, and six Catholics of varying professional backgrounds.

On June 11, 2003, Sister Marlo Damon testified in private before the review board. Listening raptly, the board heard Damon's tales of abuse she had suffered through as a child, including the alleged rapes by Chet Warren. She gave each board member a signed statement detailing charges of rape, torture, and satanic abuse that she had repressed for so long.

Damon read to the board a statement that began with personal details, explaining how her parents had moved to Toledo in her childhood years.

"We moved into St. Pius X parish where my paternal grandparents, Fred and Mary Damon were quite active. Chet Warren, then an OSFS [*Oblates of St. Francis de Sales*] priest and associate pastor befriended my family quite soon."

She went on to detail her childhood abuse at Warren's hands, charging that he made her fellate and fondle him.

"On one occasion after a Friday school liturgy, he led me into the sacristy, secured the doors and forced me to lie on my back beneath his exposed penis as he masturbated himself."

How ironic that the sacristy was also the scene of this alleged crime. The abuse she claimed progressed to violence, and by third grade, sodomy.

Then came the bombshell. Not only was Warren sexually violent, Sister Marlo claimed something worse:

"Chet Warren was a leader of a satanic group (based at St. Pius) that performed rituals in honor of Satan on a regular basis. The rituals were horrifying and sadistic, designed to break our wills and internalize whatever cores programmed message they wished to use to further our powerlessness. Among the abusers were . . . my father and grandfather."

Sister Marlo particularly remembered what happened after her beloved pet Lab Smoky died. She told the panel the story of Smoky's mutilation at the hand of her father's cult. Adding further detail, Warren allegedly told Sister Marlo if she really loved Smoky, she would be able to put him back together again and make him come back to life. Utterly confused, she cried uncontrollably. Then a cult member strode in from an adjoining room with a dog on a leash.

Warren allegedly told her of a little girl who had brought a dog back from death. "I learned that anything I loved would be annihilated and that everything was my fault."

There was a further charge that she was the victim of another ceremony at Calvary Cemetery when she was five. She was placed in a box, that to her seemed like a coffin, and cockroaches were set upon her. "They told me the bugs were marking me for Satan. I learned that I belonged to them."

Most of the rituals Sister Marlo was forced to go through included some type of sexual abuse. When she was six, she was initiated into the cult, or so she claimed. Cult members beat drums.

"Chet carried me to a table and vaginally raped me. I learned that I had no power. At age nine, Chet took me on different occasions to an old house where the cult members killed dogs. They made me crawl on the floor and pick up the dogs' innards. I learned that no matter how hard I tried, there was no way out."

In still other fantastic rituals, cult members dismembered a stillborn baby "and made me pick up the limbs." The cult also killed. After the eyeball incident, Sister Marlo claims the cult killed a little girl who was about three. After she was dead, the adults left Marlo alone "in a sea of blood and stench."

At age twelve, in yet another initiation ritual, she was given to Satan. "They used a snake and inserted it into my mouth, rectum and vagina to consecrate those orifices to Satan."

When they told her to call aloud to God, the abuse got worse. But when they told her to call aloud to Satan, the abuse stopped. She remembered and had written even more, claiming that between the ages of eight and nine she was taken someplace she didn't recognize. It was in the middle of the night. Her father, Warren, and others she did not know were there and shot pornographic pictures of her.

When she was a teenager, she was in the sacristy when a priest forced her to take off her bra, blouse and underwear, leaving on her cute uniform skirt. "He pushed me back against the sacristy counter, fondling, mouthing and kissing my breast. Then he knelt, put his head under my skirt and performed oral sex."

Chet Warren left St. Pius X suddenly in the middle of the year when Sister Marlo was in fifth grade, returning to Toledo as chaplain at St. Vincent's when Damon was in high school. "The summer between my freshman and sophomore year, I volunteered as a candy striper at St. Vincent's. Chet sexually abused me in his chaplaincy quarter several times that summer."

The abuse took place, she said, in Warren's chaplaincy quarters. Men would come and pay Chet to have sex with Damon. "These experiences included slapping, span-king, being cuffed or tied up during sex, being masked/blindfolded and having my breasts and genitals pinched or bitten during sex . . . One of these S and M perpetrators was Father Gerald Robinson, a diocesan priest. I do not know who the others were."

As a result of this repeated sexual abuse, Damon became pregnant at the age of fifteen. "The satanic group performed a cult abortion." She gave as locations for these satanic activities both some back areas of St. Pius X property and an abandoned house on Rabb Road further out in the rural section of the county.

Sister Marlo then went on to state her medical problems and as a result of this trauma to be suffering from dissociative disorder and post-traumatic stress disorder. "I have been in therapy since 1993. In 1998, my mother was in the hospital and I went home to help my dad with the laundry. While there, Chet arrived and raped me in the guest bedroom. My father also sexually assaulted me." She claimed to have "completely cut this experience off from my consciousness for several months."

Sometime during the first quarter of 2000, "I again went to my apartment, this time in a dissociated state. Again, Chet was there and again I was sexually assaulted." Later she came out of this state. When she realized she'd been assaulted, she "cut contact with my family members completely. My experiences of the past five years show me clearly that the cult is still active and dangerous."

She signed the letter "Sister Marlo Damon, SVU, 6/11/03."

Damon's recollection of her alleged rape by Father Warren is consistent with the use of the female body as the altar during the Black Mass. But what is even more interesting is that in her letter, the nun accuses her father, Robert Damon, of not only being part of the satanic ring abusing his daughter, but later selling her sexual services.

Who was Robert Damon? On April 8, 2000, the *Toledo Blade* published a human interest story about his lifelong fascination with trains.

"Some folks like to play golf or sail a boat," he told the *Blade* during the interview. "Trains just happen to be my hobby."

The article went on to describe how Damon, a retired executive with the Tana Corporation, could usually be found hanging out in his car at the Holloway Road railroad crossing, at Holland near McCord Road in Toledo. He liked to watch the trains go by.

"I've been a railroad buff since I was 5 years old," said the seventy-seven-year-old former Tana Corporation employee in the article. "I've been a train devotee for more than 70 years."

Damon enjoyed riding the rails even more, especially when accompanied by his wife, Doris, Marlo's mother. He estimated that they had taken 150 Amtrak trips since their marriage in 1948.

All this information was available to anyone in that room interested in the character of Damon's father, the alleged Satanist. All they had to do was a simple Google search; they did not. Once Damon departed for the re-

Claudia Vercellotti, SNAP's Toledo coordinator and prime mover in bringing the Robinson case to trial.

Vercellotti carries with her a display of photographs of children abused by clergy.

Dave Davison today, as he goes through the records he kept for twenty-six years before copying
them at Kinkos.

Dave Davison as a beat cop at the time of the ritualistic murder of Margaret Ann Pahl.

Courtesy Dave Davison

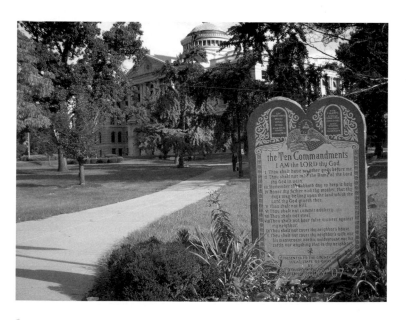

The Lucas County Courthouse where Robinson was tried in April and May 2006. Note the modern, conservative addition of the Ten Commandments in the foreground.

Sister Catherine McAuley, founder of the Sisters of Mercy, as she appears on the Irish five-pound note. It was recently replaced by the euro.

Sister Margaret Ann Pahl, right before her death.

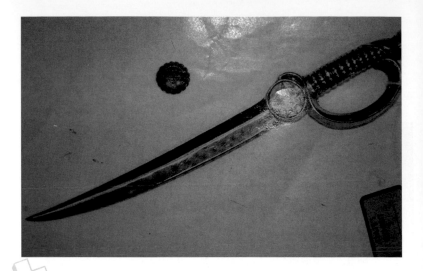

The murder weapon, Robinson's sword-shaped letter opener. Note the medallion, already removed.

A close-up of the place on the sword, under the medallion, where the forensic experts found a small spot of blood.

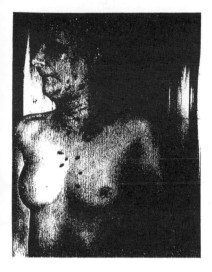 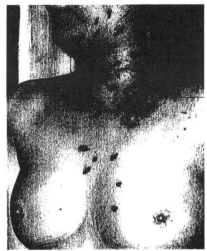

Autopsy photographs of Margaret Ann Pahl, con-
centrating on the chest wounds. Note the way the
pattern of the cross on her chest veers to the left.

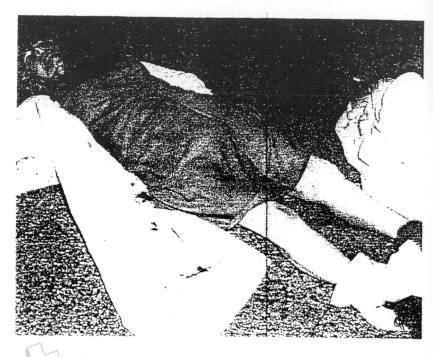
Margaret Ann Pahl as she appeared when cops first discovered her body.

view board to consider her evidence, review board member Dr. Cooley said that he wanted to report Damon's charges immediately to police because they included the murder of people used as satanic sacrifices.

Instead, the board voted five to one that Sister Marlo Damon's charges of rape, torture, and satanic abuse were not only incredible, but there wasn't cause to bring the cops in. Only Dr. Cooley thought there was. The lone holdout who believed in Damon's credibility, he had backbone.

Vercellotti and Cooley got together with Damon and told her she should go public with her charges. Still believing the Dallas Charter would get her the fifty grand and guarantee her justice, Damon refused. The diocese dragged its feet. The case languished all through the summer of 2003. In the fall, Sister Marlo Damon's patience finally wore out. The Toledo Diocese's intransigence to her problems was no longer tolerable.

She gave her champions Vercellotti and Cooley copies of her statement delivered months before to the diocese's review board. She also gave them what they had been waiting for—the green light to take her case forward to the authorities. The real question was whose trust Damon's situation would engender, or perhaps more importantly, whom Vercellotti and Cooley felt they could trust not to bury the case. The Lucas County Prosecutor's Office was low on the list and, in Vercellotti's opinion, never a viable option. Instead, Cooley and Vercellotti went directly to the state.

In September 2003, Vercellotti and Cooley met with Special Agent Phil Lucas of the Ohio Attorney General's

Office in Bowling Green. During the hour-plus meeting, they handed over to Lucas a copy of Damon's statement to the review board. Lucas requested more documentation. While Vercellotti was putting together the package of papers for the state investigator, the diocese fired Dr. Cooley from the review board. That was not surprising. After all, Cooley had refused to go along with the program. He had to go. But then, just when it seemed darkest, the system worked.

On December 2, Special Agent Lucas of the Ohio Attorney General's Office faxed a copy of Sister Marlo Damon's review board testimony to the Lucas County prosecutor, Julia Bates. He included his recommendation that an investigation be commenced immediately. The state needed to determine the veracity of Damon's charges. And just like that, Damon's charges had new life.

Since 1997, Lucas County prosecutor Julia Bates had maintained a cold case squad. Their charge was primarily to examine unsolved homicides. Using contemporary technology and old-fashioned police work, the idea was to see if they could bring resolution to these crimes. The squad was composed of personnel drawn from the Ohio Bureau of Criminal Investigation and Identification; the TPD; the county coroner and prosecutor's offices; and the FBI.

Of all the sleuths put on the case, it would be the DA's man, Tom Ross, who put the pieces together. An investigator for prosecutor Julia Bates, Ross was also a retired TPD cop. Spotting Robinson's name in Damon's letter as one of the priests accused of raping her, he immediately consulted with his colleague, Sergeant Steve Forrester of the TPD.

Ross remembered that Robinson had been the prime suspect in Pahl's murder.

Now his name had surfaced again. This time, a nun was charging Robinson raped her during years of satanic abuse that included human sacrifices. There was also a possibility of a link in some way between Robinson and Chet Warren, the main subject of Damon's charges.

Satanism was another matter.

CHAPTER 10

The Exorcist

What had stymied the TPD in its first investigation of the Pahl homicide was the deal made with the Toledo Diocese to stop before they could begin building a case against the prime suspect, Father Gerald Robinson. Despite any public statements covering their ass, the TPD was "that close" to indicting Robinson when Schmit and Vetter walked into the interrogation room and shut things down cold.

During the first years of the millennium, Dave Davison sat with his menagerie in his home on Toledo's margins, watching as a new group of young Turks took over the Toledo Police Department and replaced the old guard. That didn't mean there weren't still lots of Catholics in the TPD; there were. But the idea of masking a murder suspect, simply because he was a Catholic priest, was now abhorrent.

Because of the sexual abuse scandals across the country, Catholic priests were no longer seen as the holy men of yore. Now they were seen as *men*, just as capable of murder, child abuse, or sexual abuse as any other person. The cold case squad decided to reinvestigate the unsolved 1980 homicide of Sister Margaret Ann Pahl. The detectives were coming after Jerry Robinson. If they didn't make the case this time, the Pahl murder would probably remain unsolved forever.

On December 15, 2003, Ross and Forrester went to the diocese. In their hands was a search warrant. They met with Father Michael Billian, who functioned as the diocese's chancellor, or front man for dealing with the authorities. It happened that he and Forrester, a Catholic, were acquaintances. The warrant, they explained, was for the personnel file of Father Gerald Robinson. Robinson had been the prime suspect in the 1980 unsolved murder of Sister Margaret Ann Pahl, a case they had just reopened.

Billian went outside his office. A few minutes later, he came back in with a thin folder. It was the entire personnel file the diocese had on Robinson. Opening it, Forrester saw a personnel form with Robinson's particulars on it. A second form summarized his assignments since entering the diocese in 1964. Last was a head shot of Robinson, smiling. That was it; nothing else.

The detectives were rather surprised that after more than four decades of service to Toledo's Catholics, there wasn't more detailed information, like comments from parishioners regarding his priestly abilities, peer reviews, and some comments from the man at the top, the bishop who was Robinson's overall supervisor. For a personnel file it was pretty bare, but Billian acidulously assured the police officers that was all they had.

Something else was happening. Damon's charges of satanic abuse brought in the supernatural. While she did not place Robinson at any of the alleged satanic ceremonies in which she was the alleged victim, she did place him, and quite persuasively, in Chet Warren's room at St. Vincent's Hospital, where Warren, she claimed, prostituted her.

But it wasn't until Detective Terry Cousino examined the altar cloth lying over her chest that anyone made the charge that the murder of Margaret Ann Pahl was ritualistic. "Ritualistic" is the label homicide detectives and prosecutors like to assign to cases where they suspect satanic involvement.

Like just about everybody in Toledo who went to college, Cousino's alma mater was the hometown University of Toledo, where he got his bachelor's in art education. A member of the TPD's Scientific Investigation Unit, Cousino was a jack-of-all-trades forensic specialist. He could draw accurate composites of suspects and age them, or make a plaster of a person's face that had been shot off by a shotgun.

Cousino had more recently taken courses in a new field of forensics, bloodstain pattern transfer analysis. The theory behind bloodstain pattern transfer analysis was logical enough. A blood-soaked knife, other murder weapon, or anything at the scene coated in the red stuff, will make a distinct pattern when set down on, or when covered with something. While the field held great promise for the future, it has yet to be proven significant in obtaining regular convictions for two reasons.

First, there are only five people acknowledged worldwide as bloodstain pattern transfer analysis experts. Unless they worked for a super-secret crime-fighting organization like S.H.I.E.L.D. created by Stan Lee, they wouldn't be able to cover all the cases in one state, let alone fifty of them where their testimony could make a significant difference.

Second, unlike DNA typing, which is an objective science born out of more than fifty years of steady, dedicated research and results, bloodstain pattern transfer analysis (BPTA) is new and decidedly subjective. No matter how well-trained the specialist in this area might be, the expert must interpret, just as a frontier scout interpreted imprints in the dirt.

No matter how reliable subjectivity might be, it is not the scientific fact that DNA typing is. While law enforcement organizations try to implement standards in this new area, credible research studies need to be developed and published to answer how a subjective technique can even compare to science in weight given at trial.

This must all be taken into account, and then thrown out.

No one knows what a jury will do, and anyone who says he does is lying. A jury can be smart, like the one that convicted Harry K. Thaw in 1906 for murdering Stanford White, the first "crime of the century"; or it can be stupid, like the jury that voted to acquit O. J.

Simpson in 1995 for the last "crime of the century." Despite still being a theory, BPTA could easily be accepted by the jury and lead to conviction. Just as possible was that a good defense attorney could bring out "reasonable doubt" by arguing BTPA was not science but science fiction. Convince even one juror of that and the jury would hang.

DNA typing is 99.9 percent accurate. Bloodstain pattern transfer analysis is not. But it was all the cold case squad had. Examining the altar cloth further, Cousino noted the grouping of puncture marks in the center. There were eighteen in total, but it looked like the cloth had actually been folded over when the stabbing took place. That meant there were actually nine punctures grouped in the center of Pahl's chest.

CSI work sometimes includes using old technology. Taking a piece of tracing paper, Cousino positioned it carefully over the nine holes in the cloth. He drew lines, literally connecting the dots on the cloth that represented where the knife, he figured, had passed through and into the nun's chest. When he was finished, he announced his results to the cops.

"It's a cross," he opined.

Cousino figured the killer had used a crucifix as a template. But the stab marks were not just any cross. It was Cousino's opinion that the stab marks formed an inverted or upside-down cross, and that meant only one thing: Satan.

Devil worshippers mock Christianity using various symbols to demonstrate their displeasure with Christianity. One of these satanic symbols is the inverted cross. To a Satanist, it represents rejection and mockery of Jesus.

If such a cross were pierced into Margaret Ann's chest over her heart, the case could easily be seen as a satanically inspired ritual. Damon's charges of human sacrifice by the satanic cult could be borne out by hard evidence.

There is nothing unusual about ritual killing. It is carefully documented in a variety of cultures and is literally as old as time itself, or at least since humans first walked the earth more than one hundred thousand years ago. Many cultures that have long since become history, including the Mayans, the Incas, and others, ritually killed human beings, usually for some sort of sacrifice to appease one god or another.

The Catholic Church crystallized the concept of the Devil or Satan in Mathew 25:41, "the Devil and his angels," giving their chief or head fallen angel the name Lucifer. Thereafter, ritual killing involved in many instances worshipping Lucifer. But as time passed and cultures became more and more educated and enlightened, such ideas fell by the transom of history.

By the twentieth century, ritual killing was practically nonexistent in the United States. Public perception changed with the publication of Ira Levin's 1967 best-seller *Rosemary's Baby*, which brought devil worshipping to the masses. It was a frightening story of a devil-worshipping cult in modern-day Manhattan, composed of people just like you and me, who just happened to implant a nice girl named Rosemary with Satan's spawn.

Under Roman Polanski's absolutely brilliant direction,

the 1968 screen version became an instant classic that transcended the bounds of its own horror genre. Through Rosemary's travails, it indelibly stamped images of ritualistic sexual abuse on the American consciousness. Then, as if to prove out his own thesis, Polanski showed how easy it was to become a victim of devil worshipping in his own life.

Polanski's wife, Sharon Tate, was the most well-known victim of Charles Manson and his devil-worshipping cult that killed six people on two consecutive nights, August 8 to 9, 1969. The subsequent trial lasted from 1970 to 1971, and prosecutor Vincent Bugliosi's 1975 account of the case, *Helter Skelter*, focused the public's attention once more on ritual killing.

As the Manson case showed, Satanism is about sex and power. Under the guise of worshipping Satan, felons rape, beat, and psychologically abuse those they make part of their ritual. Charlie Manson, for example, controlled his cult by making them believe he was the Devil incarnate. Yet he was nothing more than a charismatic, insane con man who had spent more than half of his miserable life behind bars.

David Berkowitz, who in 1977 was arrested in Westchester, New York, for being the self-described serial killer the Son of Sam, admitted he was part of a satanic cult. Though police played this down at the time, evidence developed later that there could have been more than one "shooter," from Berkowitz's cult. As late as 1997 during a nationally televised interview, Berkowitz told Larry King that he had belonged to a devil-worshipping cult.

Sister Margaret Ann Pahl's death could have been part of a satanic ritual performed by Father Robinson. Evidence of the rituals themselves would help corroborate Damon's statement. Confusing matters, there were some writers and cops who considered themselves self-styled Satanism experts. If there was even a hint of satanic activity, they never failed to seize the media spotlight and flog the Satanism angle to death in order to sell themselves and their points of view.

Homicide cops don't like to admit it, but more often than not, they form a theory of the crime. Then they gather the evidence with an eye toward supporting that theory, rather than going where the evidence leads. Sometimes it works and sometimes it doesn't.

Right from the beginning in 1980, the TPD cops formed the theory that Father Gerald Robinson had killed Sister Margaret Ann Pahl. He was the only suspect. The cops figured he strangled her with his hands and then used his letter opener to stab her to death, having laid the altar cloth over her chest first. Tying the letter opener and the altar cloth to the crime was therefore essential.

Forrester and Ross pulled all the evidence from the 1980 homicide. They asked Daniel Davison of the Ohio Bureau of Criminal Investigation to see what he could find out about the letter opener. Using contemporary science, Ross could not connect the letter opener to Pahl's body. He could not say one way or the other whether it was Robinson's letter opener that punctured Margaret Ann Pahl's skin.

"I had Steve Ross call me for a DNA test," says Dave

Davison. "I asked him why and he said they were trying to rule out everyone who was at the crime as being the perpetrator."

Davison, though, didn't trust Ross or the TPD.

"I refused. He said if I didn't get my ass down there and give them a swab, he would get a court order. I told him to go ahead."

As part of the case he was building against Robinson, assistant prosecutor Dean Mandros subpoenaed the following from St. Vincent's Hospital Pathology Department:

". . . you are hereby commanded to release tissue in paraffin block and glass slides from the 1995 medical treatment and surgery at Mercy Hospital of Father Jerome Swiatecki to the Lucas Count Prosecuting Attorney's Office."

Father Swiatecki had had some surgery in the mid-nineties at the hospital, which had stored his tissue samples inside paraffin for long-term convenience. The prosecution could use it to type his DNA and compare it to any gathered at the crime scene, and thus rule him out. The cops then asked for voluntary DNA samples from as many of the people who were at the 1980 crime scene as they could find.

Davison's reticence to allow the TPD access to his genetic code was well-founded. The department needed to prove to honest veterans like Davison that the go-to boys no longer controlled the department, that everyone, including Catholic priests, was subject to criminal prosecution for felonious acts that not only defied common criminal law, they defied canon law as well.

None of the DNA typing made a difference anyway. What little blood that was on the letter opener, under where the medallion used to be, had been tested back in 1980, and had proved too little to even blood type, e.g., A, B. By the time they came to Cousino, the TPD cops were running out of options.

With Cousino's information regarding blood pattern transfer analysis in hand, they proceeded to get two of the five world experts on bloodstain pattern transfer analysis to agree to testify for the prosecution: T. Paulette Sutton and Dr. Henry Lee. Both experts would say that Robinson's letter opener pierced the altar cloth, the blood leaving a distinct pattern of an inverted cross on the cloth.

The meaning of the stab wounds was crucial to the prosecution of the case. If Cousino was right in his interpretation, they needed an expert on ritualistic killings. TPD detectives found themselves traveling to Chicago, just three and a half hours away from Toledo by car, to ask for the assistance of the one man who could help: the exorcist.

Father Jeffrey Grob is the assistant exorcist and director of canonical services for the Archdiocese of Chicago.

"I sort of backed into it because of the dissertation I was working on at the time on the rite of exorcism," says Father Grob.

The archdiocese had a hole that it needed to fill, and Father Grob got the call. It was not surprising. Father Grob, who also has a Ph.D. in canon law, is the real deal. Warm, eloquent, and self-effacing, he heads up the Office of Canonical Services for the Archdiocese of Chicago.

"I perform a wide range of activities for the Chicago Archdiocese. Any question pertaining to church or canon law comes to me. An additional duty because of my dissertation on exorcism is that any call regarding matters of the occult, where someone claims possession, is routed to me. I'm the front person for anyone who has a problem regarding evil manifesting itself in people. I backed into the role when I was writing a Ph.D. on the Catholic rite of exorcism in 1999."

Regarding calls from people claiming to be possessed or knowing people who are, Father Grob answers, "Usually most problems can be resolved right on the phone. You must understand that an exorcist is trained to be a skeptic. Most of these [possession] situations involve people who are psychotic, exhibit bipolar behavior, schizophrenia. That's why it's very important to know what's actually going on in a person's life. A great many matters can be resolved quickly."

If not, Grob could be called upon to do what he has done in the past—a full-blown exorcism.

"It's actually a prayer service where you are praying with the person afflicted. I can tell you that most [cases of possession] are extremely rare," Grob reveals.

For the Pahl homicide, the TPD contacted and worked with him as their expert witness on ritualistic killings.

"I went back and forth to Toledo, a number of times over a period of about three years," says Father Grob. During that time, the prosecution and defense were building their cases and going through pretrial motions.

"My primary focus was on working with the team of detectives from Toledo. I viewed all the evidence, the autopsy photos, the piece of linen. At first glance, it looked like random stabbings. But then, it looked like there was something more to it. It was the nature of the stab wounds. It became evident there was a pattern to the markings on the cloth."

"Any of these things individually can be just that, what they are. It's in the conglomerate that makes something a ritual. It was the grouping. The mark on the forehead was a mockery of the anointing of the sick. It would be a particular mockery to a Sister of Mercy who is dedicated to extreme unction."

Father Grob was very much aware of the hill the prosecution would have to climb with the jury pool.

"If you think it's difficult now to grasp the idea of a priest being a man long enough to accept that if he is, he's capable of murder like anyone else, can you imagine what 1980 was like? It was simply unthinkable," Father Grob continues.

While the murder investigation against Father Robinson was reaching its zenith in 2004, a parallel investigation was also going on by the TPD.

The cops were looking into Sister Marlo Damon's accusations of physical and sexual abuse by a satanic cult operating in Lucas County. What they needed was hard, prosecutorial evidence. This time, there would be no cover-ups. Police looked at a dilapidated, abandoned house on Raab Road in western Lucas County. It matched the description of the Raab Road house where

Damon said in her statement she was gang-raped by a group of Satanists in the 1970s. Police could not find any evidence that the house had been a cult gathering place. There was no blood, no bones, no skin, no graves around the place, no indication whatsoever that the place was anything other than what it seemed to be.

Police now had all kinds of chemicals and instruments popularized on the TV show *CSI* that could be used to find evidence of a crime. Police checked the local churches where Damon claimed the group operated. They went into the basement of Pope Pius X, where Chet Warren had been a pastor and led some of his satanic activities, according to Damon.

They checked out the basement of Holy Trinity Church in Richfield Center, Ohio, another location for the cult that Damon had identified as a satanic site. They also looked at a residence used by Oblates priests on Parkwood Avenue that matched another description from Damon's statement; again, they could find no evidence to support her claims.

What the police were left with regarding physical evidence of a satanic cult operating in Lucas County was nothing. That didn't mean Damon's abuse didn't happen. It might very well have and Robinson could have been party to it. But a prosecutor would be tempting fate to put Sister Marlo Damon on the stand.

The troubling diagnosis was at the end of her statement. Damon says she suffers from PTSS, which usually goes with dissociative disorder. Dissociative disorder is best known under the layman's term "split personality."

The nation's largest grassroots mental health organization, the National Alliance on Mental Health (NAMI), reports that dissociative disorders "are so-called because they are marked by a dissociation from or interruption of a person's fundamental aspects of waking consciousness (such as one's personal identity, one's personal history, etc.).

"Dissociative disorders come in many forms, the most famous of which is dissociative identity disorder, formerly known as *multiple personality disorder* [author emphasis]. All of the dissociative disorders are thought to stem from trauma experienced by the individual with this disorder."

Given the nature of its barbarity, the abuse Damon claimed as a child and teenager would easily suffice to provoke a split personality, in order to just cope with the ongoing trauma.

"The dissociative aspect is thought to be a coping mechanism—the person literally dissociates himself from a situation or experience too traumatic to integrate with his conscious self. Symptoms of these disorders, or even one or more of the disorders themselves, are also seen in a number of other mental illnesses, including post-traumatic stress disorder, panic disorder, and obsessive compulsive disorder," NAMI continues.

Damon was chief witness to Robinson's alleged abuse and rape. Her anonymity would be blown if she was called as a witness at the priest's trial. That assumed, of course, that he was eventually charged with murder and there was an actual trial. If that happened, the prosecution would have to make a difficult decision. Putting on the stand a witness who has dissociative disorder immediately opens up a defense challenge to the witness's psychological competence.

A good defense attorney would first make it a point that the jury understand that the person making the charges, despite being a nun, was also a split personality. Who was making the charges? Personality A, Personality B, or someone else? A good defense attorney would raise this question with the jury:

"How can you believe someone who makes charges of satanic abuse that are not provable by hard evidence, let alone a charge against a priest that he raped her?" That, of course would be the danger in putting Damon on the stand. If the defense damaged her credibility, it would, in turn, damage the credibility of the charges against Robinson.

That, though, would be the prosecutor's problem. For now, police needed to stick to building their case. They put cops on Robinson to tail him to make sure he didn't try to leave town before being charged and to get used to his routine so that when they were ready to charge him, they would know where he was.

While all of this was going on, the ink-stained wretches of the media had finally glommed onto the case. On April 23, 2004, TV satellite trucks and newspaper reporters showed up at Robinson's home. He had a small house on Nebraska Avenue, where he used to nurse his ill mother. When she died, he stayed on. With the media there now, their suspect might not just turn rabbit; he might destroy evidence if indeed he was the "bad guy" the cops were seeking.

Forrester got a search warrant from Lucas County

Common Pleas Court Judge Robert Christiansen. Armed with that warrant, he and Ross drove over to search the priest's home. Robinson opened the screen door of his home just enough to see the badges Forrester and Ross showed him. He let them in, and they chatted in his musty living room.

The cops explained they were there as part of a reinvestigation of Sister Margaret Ann Pahl's homicide in 1980. Then they went through the usual litany of questions: "Do you know anyone who would want to harm her? Did she have any enemies," et al. Of course, it was all a feint for the real stuff, which didn't take long in coming.

For the next few hours, the cops did a back-and-forth with Robinson, peppering him with questions that made it absolutely clear that they thought he was the killer. After this questioning, they finally decided to formally charge him with first-degree murder, which was what the whole charade was about in the first place. Robinson was placed under arrest for murder and advised of his constitutional rights, aka the Miranda warning that every viewer of any TV cop show knows by heart. Making matters worse, Forrester showed him the warrant. While he was being charged with murder the cops would be shaking down his place. Without putting on the cuffs, Ross escorted him out the front door, leaving his partner behind.

During the search, the cops found pictures of dead people, but not just any dead people. They were death photos of people in their coffins. The photos ranged from daguerreotypes from the early part of the twentieth century to up-to-date digital shots. They also found a pamphlet entitled *The Occult*. Published by a Catholic group, it was found on one of the priest's bookshelves.

The pamphlet was shopworn from overuse. Some passages were highlighted in yellow; there were handwritten notes in the margins. While the pamphlet was standard issue to priests in the 1970s, Robinson had kept it through many moves. That alone did not mitigate toward his guilt. Many other priests, of course, possessed the same booklet in their bookshelves. None of them, however, was the prime suspect in the murder of a nun with ritualistic overtones.

CHAPTER 11

Arrest . . .

April 23, 2004

Coincidentally, there was a police precinct next door to Robinson's home. The cop and the priest suspected of murder walked the few steps to the old precinct house. Even Warner Bros. had never imagined that teaming. Inside the precinct, the desk sergeant got about the paperwork of charging a man for murder. He also freed up an interrogation room for the detective.

Cops like to call them interview rooms, but they're not. Police techniques of interrogation have vastly improved over the years; not the least of the improvements is the regular absence of force. But any way you cut it, it was still an interrogation room. The third degree, the bright light shining in a suspect's face while the detectives shout hostile questions, has been replaced by police officers who are specially trained in the art of interrogation. They have taken college courses; attended FBI special training seminars and Homeland Security Department interrogation briefings; and studied a wide variety of articles on the fine art of getting the suspect to give you what you want.

It all starts with convincing the suspect to sign a waiver of his constitutional rights, allowing him to be interrogated without a lawyer being present. Ross got Robinson to sign the document. That allowed Ross to proceed without having to worry that something the priest said could be excluded. With the waiver signed, unless Robinson verbally invoked his right to a lawyer, which would stop the interrogation instantly, anything else he said would be used to hang him.

Ross did a few preliminary feints with background questions—what was it like working at the hospital, what were his duties, stuff like that before getting to how Robinson found out Sister Margaret Ann had been killed.

"Well, I had just gotten out of the shower," said Robinson.

He was toweling off when the phone rang in his small efficiency. Picking up the phone from its cradle, he put the receiver to his ear.

"Father, this is Sister Phyllis Ann. Sister Margaret Ann has been killed! Come to the sacristy and quickly!"

Robinson got dressed in his priest's uniform of cassock, white shirt, collar, black pants, and black shoes.

Walking as quickly as he could—he explained to the cop that he couldn't run in a priest's cassock—he got to the sacristy in time to see Sister Margaret Ann's body.

"Father Swiatecki was already there and some of the nuns." Then, Robinson volunteered, "Father said to me, 'Why did you do this? Why did you do it?'"

Because it was a statement from left field, it left Robinson mystified; he failed to respond. Then, perhaps picking up on the non sequitur, Robinson attempted some blame of his own. He proceeded to state that Swiatecki was an alcoholic. Of course, he failed to divulge that he himself had a drinking problem.

Ross was a good interrogator.

"Was he [Swiatecki] drunk in the sacristy when he said that to you?"

"No," Robinson explained, "he was in AA."

In going over the old reports of the homicide, Ross explained that he had come upon statements from hospital employees who claimed they had heard suspicious footsteps running *away* from the chapel at the time of the murder. One witness even claimed the footsteps stopped just short of Father Robinson's door.

Robinson just shook his head.

"I was in the shower, I couldn't hear anything."

Ross went for the kill. He pulled out a photo of the punctured altar cloth.

"We have experts who will testify that your letter opener fits the puncture marks in this cloth," he said, passing the picture over to Robinson. "Father, your letter opener matches the puncture wounds through the altar cloth. Why is that?"

Robinson had no answer. Ross pulled out a photo of the bloodstains on the altar cloth over the chest. He passed that one over too.

"We have experts who will testify that those bloodstains match your letter opener."

Again, Robinson had no answer.

After almost two hours of interrogation, the cops had gotten almost nothing. Robinson was not going to make some dramatic confession; that much was sure. His lack of emotion meant that he could not be rattled by conventional interrogation methods. It was therefore time to get down to it.

Ross finished the interrogation. He had Robinson stand, cuffed his hands, and had him taken downtown for formal booking and a little stint behind bars until, and unless, he made bail. Part of that process was turning over the contents of his pockets at the city jail. In Robinson's case, in his wallet was the card of Hank Herschel, the diocese lawyer who had entered the interrogation room in 1980.

Surely the Toledo Diocese would have the decency to provide an attorney for one of its own. They had done so in 1980, and there was no reason they wouldn't in the millennium. Robinson was certainly owed that courtesy. After all, priests take a vow of poverty to serve the church. Instead, the Toledo Diocese went into "damage control mode," which is a synonym for lying.

On Saturday April 24, 2004, the Toledo Diocese publicly stated, "No sexual abuse allegations were ever made against Robinson." Of course they had! Sister Marlo Damon appeared before the Toledo Diocesan Review Board on June 11, 2003, during which appearance she implicated Robinson as one of her rapists. That had been kept private.

The next day the diocese came back with the public statement that Damon's allegations were "not formal." In response, Claudia Vercellotti mobilized SNAP, which was keeping Damon's identity a secret. The Sister of Cathedral was known to most of the media as "Sister Jane Doe." A few select reporters on the *Toledo Blade* also knew her identity but would not divulge it.

SNAP refuted the diocese's charge that Damon's allegations weren't formal by simply pointing out that when Damon appeared before the review board, it was with a written statement, copies of which were distributed to all board members.

On Monday, April 26, 2004, the diocese turned around and claimed that Damon's allegations weren't sexual in nature. That was a new one. Vercellotti pointed out that the whole purpose of the review board, according to the Dallas Charter, was not only to hear sexual abuse cases, it was to protect children per the bishops' word-of-honor promise.

The diocese came back the next day, Tuesday, April 27, 2004, with the assertion that neither Damon nor her allegations were credible. SNAP responded: No one ever advised "Jane" as such. To reinforce the diocese's position, on April 28, Bishop Leonard Blair, the current bishop, told the press that Damon never made "sexual abuse allegations that involved Robinson."

The next day April 29, the bishop's office issued a retraction, saying, "perhaps he'd been misinformed."

That's what Rick Blaine (Humphrey Bogart) tells Major Strasser in *Casablanca* when Strasser asks him why he came to the Moroccan town.

"For the waters," says Rick.

"But there are no waters in Casablanca," Strasser counters.

Rick, a cynical man, puffs his cigarette nonchalantly and says, "I was misinformed." And you know he wasn't; not this guy.

For its part, the Lucas County prosecutor, now convinced Robinson had killed Pahl back in 1980, would bring the weight of the state to bear on the impending contest. They would continue to make its case, and one of the good things about being the state is that you have a big public coffer from which to draw funds for your prosecution.

The prosecution already had something on Robinson that Ross had gotten during his interrogation of the priest. In the 1980 account of the investigation was a statement that Swiatecki had turned to Robinson and said, "Why did you do this?" Now Robinson himself not only verified that account to Ross, he had volunteered that incriminating statement, knowing full well anything he said would be used against him; he signed a waiver to that effect. He had no explanation for why Swiatecki thought him a murderer, nor was any necessary.

"Let others debate and conclude. I am just an instrument of the law," said Lieutenant Philip Gerard, brilliantly played by Barry Morse in TV's *The Fugitive*.

It was as truthful a statement as anyone could make

about a police officer working on a circumstantial murder case.

INDICTMENT

THE STATE OF OHIO,
Lucas County, } ss.

Of the May, Term of 2004, A.D.

    THE JURORS OF THE GRAND JURY of the State of Ohio, within and for Lucas County, Ohio, on their oaths, in the name and by the authority of the State of Ohio, do find and present that GERALD ROBINSON, on or about the 5th day of April, 1980, in Lucas County, Ohio, did purposely, and with prior calculation and design, cause the death of another, in violation of §2903.01(A) OF THE OHIO REVISED CODE, AGGRAVATED·MURDER. contrary to the form of the statute in such case made and provided, and against the peace and dignity of the State of Ohio.

Julia R. Bates
Lucas County Prosecutor

    Arresting a priest and charging him with the murder of a nun, even in a backwater Midwest city like Toledo, is big news. "Father Gerald Robinson" became a major search term on Google, bringing up 44,300 worldwide hits. The priest indicted for killing the nun was major news in Africa, Asia, Australia, Europe, England, and everyplace in between. And then came the cable news charge.

Court TV was ready to offer a modest form of sensationalism, gavel-to-gavel coverage of the trial. That, of course, meant ratings. Some executive must have been rubbing his hands somewhere, hoping the defense would be stupid enough to have the priest try on a glove that was left at the murder scene or some spectacle like that played out on live TV.

Over on CNN's *News Night with Aaron Brown*, Brown, one of the most astute and compassionate anchors in television history, tried to offer a look at the crime in the context of the priestly abuse scandals that had rocked the country. At his regular mid-hour break, Brown offered real existential perspective—the latest list of the dead soldiers in Iraq, backed up by soft, somber music.

Brown didn't get the ratings. He was drowned out by the other cable news channels, the tabloids, and the TV "news magazines" that flocked like vultures to feed off Margaret Ann Pahl's flesh. If any of them were interested in actually bringing any answers to the case, or some sort of closure to Pahl's family, it got lost in the big carnival.

DNA forensic technology had not existed in 1951 or in 1980 when it could have been used to match body fluids present on or in Margaret Ann's body. In 2004, that technology not only existed, it was proven fact. The prosecution figured if they could find some DNA on Margaret Ann's body that matched Robinson's, they had him cold. Problem was, she wasn't above ground.

There she was, buried under six feet of dirt in a coffin encased in an airtight concrete vault someplace in Fremont, Ohio. Whatever was left inside tempted the prosecutors with DNA heaven. Without first informing defense attorneys of their intentions, Lucas County prosecutor Julia Bates issued an order of exhumation.

She was playing the prosecution's ace in the hole.

On May 20, 2004, a posse of lawmen led by Ross and Cousino, joined by civilians representing the Sisters of Mercy, descended on Margaret Ann's grave in Fremont, Ohio. The last time she had been above ground, the weather had been wet and windy. That day was wet all right, with the air feeling like a damp wool coat, about to rain at any moment, but for some reason, holding off.

Cemetery workers turned over the six feet of impacted dirt with spades and shovels, working carefully. They did not want to take the chance of damaging the vault. Soon, their shovels struck something solid in the dirt. Ropes were thrown down and attached. The vault, with the casket inside, was lifted whole out of the ground by the workers and placed gently on the green lawn of the cemetery.

Using crowbars, the workers pried up the lid. Looking inside, they saw that Margaret Ann Pahl's pine casket was barely intact. Placed on a wide flower tray, it was transported to the Lucas County Coroner's Office, arriving there at 1 P.M. on May 20. At the beginning of her examination, Diane Scala-Barnett, M.D., forensic pathologist and deputy coroner who was performing the second autopsy, saw that the side rail handles had come away from the coffin body and were dangling off. Noting that the soft, fiberboard casket itself had collapsed, the ME added a further element of earthiness with the observation that black and yellow mold covered parts of the waterlogged casket.

Removing the lid, Scala-Barnett had a problem; it stuck under Margaret Ann's right arm. Upon further examination, she found that the body had been propped up by an empty "All Purpose" Frigid brand container. Also in the coffin was a more thoughtful pillow someone had carefully placed under Margaret Ann's head.

Margaret Ann's face was covered by a black veil. Lifting it gently, the ME saw that Margaret Ann's features were covered with thick white mold. She wore a pair of black framed glasses. Her gray hair was still attached to her scalp. For some of the tests, Scala-Barnett had in mind, she got a break.

Margaret Ann's skin had not decomposed; it was, instead, thick and hard. The ME supervised as the body was removed from the coffin and placed onto a gurney in a body bag. Sister Pahl had been dressed for her funeral in a blue long-sleeved habit with a stand-up collar and veil. Rosary beads surrounded her hands, which were crossed over her abdomen. Carefully, the ME removed the rosary and found that it contained not one but two crosses. There was a tarnished metal ring on the fourth finger of her left hand.

Even in death, Margaret Ann dressed properly, in ribbed nylon pantyhose, slip, and panties underneath her habit. Removing the clothes, the ME discovered her body covered by the same thick white mold that covered her face. The stuff extended over the clothing as well as the stockings. Overall, the body "appears quite dehydrated and mummified."

The ME scraped most of the mold away "from the region of the left neck and thorax. The stab wounds are readily apparent, they are now dry and shriveled. The jaw is exposed and molars from the left side of the jaw are removed for submission to BCI for DNA purposes. Pubic hair standards and head hair standards are also removed and these items are given to Ms. Stacy Shipman, representative of the Bureau of Criminal Identification."

Next, Scala-Barnett reopened the Y-shaped classical incision that went from the thorax to the pubic bone. Examining the nun's insides, she found nothing different from Dr. Fazekas's 1980 autopsy. But that was 1980 and this was 2004. Scala-Barnett and forensic anthropologist Julie Saul did some interesting things to Margaret Ann's body over the following week.

Working together, the two medical professionals "tediously removed soft tissue from bone in the areas of the left jaw and preauticular [ear] area, cervical vertebrae, manubrium, sternum and anterior runs. A total of six boney defects were revealed."

Depending on your point of view, prosecution or defense, what happen next was either a brilliant piece of new police technology or old-fashioned voodoo hoodoo. The two scientists took the priest's letter opener and "we examined and compared the similarities of the suspected weapon to the boney defects. The suspected weapon was introduced into three of the boney defects as well as the cartilaginous interface. The suspected weapon was an *exact fit* [author emphasis] from all angles."

Scala-Barnett concluded:

"It is my opinion, from my examination of the first autopsy photographs, the stab wounds in the skin, and by my examination of the boney defects at the end of the stab wounds path recovered at the second autopsy, that the weapon in question, the dagger letter opener with the Washington, DC insignia, is an instrument identical to the shape and size of this, and has caused these wounds."

Dated June 10, 2004, Scala-Barnett signed the three-page single-spaced report. Copies were delivered to the cops and prosecutors working the case. A copy was also delivered to defense attorney John Thebes. Shortly after Robinson's arrest, John Thebes took his case. Thebes knew Father Robinson from his second grade class at Christ the King where Robinson served as the second pastor out of three from 1969 to 1972. Approached by Robinson's family to represent him, he agreed. A Roman Catholic, Thebes did not think his client a murderer.

Pending trial, Robinson was arraigned. The judge set him free on a $200,000 bond. Robinson had no money, but his supporters did. After his arrest, they came forth in the hundreds, putting up their homes for collateral. They crowded around him when he was released on bail on May 3, slapping him on the back like he was a rock star. These were people who had been parishioners in Robinson's churches over the years and found him to be a decent, kind fellow.

Soon, three more lawyers came aboard to help the father fight the first-degree murder charge. There were John Callahan, silver-haired, elegantly dressed, the dean of Toledo attorneys; Michelle Khoury, a twenty-eight-year-old criminal defense attorney with two acquittals to her credit; and Alan Konop, a veteran defense attorney with a coiffed white beard and piercing dark eyes highlighted by an ever-present set of glasses worn at the end of his nose.

All of Gerald Robinson's attorneys worked pro bono.

Robinson's supporters had fund-raisers to help pay for the other expenses his defense would engender, including fees for expert witnesses. The weight of the state might be bearing down on Father Robinson's frail shoulders, but as far as his former parishioners were concerned, the father had God on his side and he would eventually be proven innocent.

For its part, the state was moving forward. Forrester had done some research and discovered that a Catholic diocese is required under canon law to maintain secret archives of any criminal investigation. Confronted with this information, Father Billian at the diocese denied the existence of such an archive in Toledo. This time, the cops didn't trust him. Forrester and Ross put together a no-knock search warrant allowing them to search the diocese's headquarters for those secrets, signed by Judge Robert Christiansen of Lucas County Common Pleas Court. They served it at diocesan headquarters, Catholic Center, on September 15, 2004.

Father Billian happened to be out at the time. Another priest, confronted with the no-knock warrant, took the cops to a file room. He left them alone for a few minutes and then came back with a thick manila folder. Inside were scores of documents about Robinson's service to the diocese.

The cops came back with a second no-knock warrant two days later on September 17, allowing them to search Billian's office for his records on Robinson. This time, they came away with nothing. Wherever the secret archives were, they appeared destined to remain that way. Bishop Blair made a public statement that despite "the claim that the church's Code of Canon Law says that dioceses should maintain a secret archive," Toledo not only didn't have one, as far as Blair knew, one had probably never existed in the past either.

Blair failed to explain why, if the diocese was so cooperative with the police, the cops needed not one, not two, but *three* search warrants, two within days of each other, to search Catholic Center. Then again, it wasn't Blair who was going on trial.

What with pretrial motions and postponements of one sort or another, the wheels of justice in Toledo move ever so slowly.

September 8, 2005

The fire burned white hot, melting the sides of two fire trucks dispatched to contain it. With the wind at its back, the flames turned, burning six homes to the ground in a matter of minutes. While any fire can burn hot and cold in spots, one that gets to white hot destroys all evidence. Nothing survives.

That's a good thing if you're an arsonist.

It started in the rear apartment of 2425 Broadway, beside the Maumee River about half a mile from the Toledo Zoo. The apartment was rented to SNAP's Toledo leader, Claudia Vercellotti. Before the fire, Vercellotti was lying on the bed in her bedroom. On the other end of the phone line was her mother. Claudia was trying to justify begging off a not-very-important doctor's appointment.

Her mother urged her to go. After hanging up, Claudia lay there in the early evening twilight. She could hear the boats on the river. It was soothing and restful. That damn appointment, she thought, feeling the guilt pangs of a child who knows her parent is right.

"So I stood up, scooped my wallet and keys up that were on the piano." Also on the piano was the urn containing her father's ashes. "I just went to the door and I walked out. There was nothing that told me this was forever. There was nothing unusual, nothing out of place."

Claudia left to make her doctor's appointment. This time, the guilt saved her life. Forty-three minutes later, at about 4:43 P.M., firemen later estimated, Vercellotti's apartment was on fire, and with it, eighteen file drawers of collected research and insider documents, many of which had never been made public. Most of the documents pertained to cases of priests sexually abusing minors.

The day after the fire, Vercellotti sorted through the ashes. "Everything was gone. Everything . . ." But she searched within the ashes for her father's remains in the urn that had sat atop the piano. She never found it.

"I am only left with questions and no answers. I was there tonight, I deeply miss the water. There are large slabs of concrete there, from the dig on the first property that is being rebuilt. It's surreal, really. My heart still races when I drive up the street. I am undergoing a lot of delayed grieving.

"I can't tell you it was arson and they can't tell me it wasn't—and I can't afford to believe one over the other. It's hard to think though, that anyone deemed me a threat. The diocese really looked at me as a nuisance, a mild nuisance—like the fly at the picnic that won't go away."

December 24, 2005

IN THE COMMON PLEAS COURT OF LUCAS COUNTY, OHIO

COMMON PLEAS COURT
BERNIE QUILTER No. CR04-1915
CLERK OF COURTS

STATE OF OHIO

    Plaintiff,

    -vs-

GERALD ROBINSON

    Defendant

*   Hon. Thomas J. Osowik

*   <u>MOTION TO AMEND</u>
<u>INDICTMENT</u>

*

*   Dean P. Mandross, #0016641
    Assistant Prosecuting Attorney
*   Lucas County Courthouse
    Toledo, Ohio 43624
*   Phone: (419) 213-4700
    Fax: (419) 213-4595

Now comes the State of Ohio, by and through Assistant Prosecuting Attorney Dean P.

Mandross, and moves this Court to amend the indictment against the Defendant to delete

reference to Defendant acting "with prior calculation and design."

Crim. R. 7(D) provides in relevant part:

"The court may at any time before, during, or after a trial amend the indictment, information, complaint, or bill of particulars, in respect to any defect, imperfection, or omission in form or substance, or of any variance with the evidence, provided no change is made in the name or identity of the crime charged."

Crim. R. 7 (D) also allows that if the amendment changes the identity of the crime charged—as

herein from aggravated murder to murder—the Defendant would be entitled to discharge a

sitting jury and request a reasonable continuance. Such measures are obviously not required here

where the trial is still four months away.

Additionally the Ohio Supreme Court has ruled that the original indictment may be amended even during the trial if the amended charge is a lesser included offense of the original

charge. *State v. Briscoe* (1992), 84 Ohio App.3d 569, 617. Such is the case here where the

amended charge, murder, is a lesser included offense of the original charge, aggravated murder.

As such, the State of Ohio moves to amend the subject indictment in case no. CR04-1915

to read as follows:

> "The jurors of the grand jury of the State of Ohio, within and for Lucas County,
> Ohio, on their oaths, in the name and by the authority of the State of Ohio, do find
> and present that GERALD ROBINSON, on or about the 5th day of April, 1980, in
> Lucas County, Ohio, did purposely cause the death of another, in violation of §
> 2903.02(A) of the Ohio Revised Code, Murder, contrary to the form of the statute
> in such case made and provided, and against the peace and dignity of the State of
> Ohio."

For the foregoing reasons, the State respectfully requests that this Court grant the State's

motion to amend the current indictment to delete reference to Defendant acting with prior

calculation and design.

Respectfully submitted,

JULIA R. BATES, PROSECUTING ATTORNEY
LUCAS COUNTY, OHIO

By: _____
Dean P. Mandross, # 0016641
Assistant Prosecuting Attorney

Vercellotti vastly underestimated her importance. Without her lobbying for Sister Damon with the state, there would have been no prosecution of Gerald Robinson for murder. It had been Detective Ross who noticed Robinson's name in Damon's statement, but it was Vercellotti who got the statement into the right hands. While the TPD had yet to get back to Damon regarding an investigation into the rape allegations against Robinson, it was easy to see that a murder indictment trumped a rape indictment any day of the week.

Assistant prosecutor Dean Mandros won a lot more than he lost. Just like every other attorney on this case, and on most cases in Lucas County, Mandros had graduated from the University of Toledo School of Law. The place was so popular locally, it ought to do a public offering.

They taught Mandros well. Amending a charge of first-degree murder or, as it's known in Ohio, "aggravated murder," to the lower charge of "murder" meant that Mandros did not have to prove premeditation. The penalty for "aggravated murder" was twenty to life. The penalty for "murder" was fifteen to life. In Ohio, there was no time off for good behavior. The minimum was the minimum.

Trading five years behind bars for a sixty-eight-year-old in poor physical condition for a better shot at convicting him seemed like a good deal. Yet, despite its confident public stance on getting a conviction against a priest, the Lucas County Prosecutor's Office knew it would not be easy.

It never is, when it hasn't been done before.

CHAPTER 12

... and Trial

April 21, 2006

After almost two years of behind-the-scenes legal wrangling over everything from purported audio statements Robinson had made in 1980 to the accuracy of blood transfer analysis evidence, the trial of Father Gerald Robinson for the 1980 murder of Sister Margaret Ann Pahl was finally ready to begin. It had only taken twenty-six years.

The decedent was back in her grave, hopefully never to be bothered again. Margaret Ann's body had been redressed in a fresh habit and her eyeglasses repositioned over her now mold-free face. Her rosary with the two crosses was carefully placed back in her mummified hands. The morgue attendants then placed the body of the woman who was born in 1909 and died in 1980, in an ambulance that transported her to the Keller-Ochs-Koch Funeral Home. From there, Margaret Ann Pahl was taken back to her grave, hopefully for the final time.

Judge Thomas Osowik's second-floor wood-paneled courtroom was filled to overflowing. A fourteen-person jury had gone through voir dire and been seated. To their left were two large tables. The one nearer was the prosecution's. Mandros, the chief of the criminal division, took first chair. He was assisted by Larry Kiroff, who had ten years' experience as a civil litigator for the feds and the city; and forensics expert J. Christopher Anderson.

Farther away from the jury was the defense table. Dressed in his clerical habit, despite an order from the diocese that he wear "civvies," was the frail, white-haired figure of Gerald Robinson, surrounded by his "Fantastic Four." The courtroom of Judge Osowik was filled to overflowing. No surprise considering what was happening outside.

Usually vacant hotel rooms were filled to capacity. The restaurants, even the lousy ones, had lots of business. The big carnival had descended once more on Toledo. The longer the trial of the priest went on, the bigger the ratings, the more ads the cable channels would sell, and the more Toledo's businesses prospered. Lord knew they needed something.

In 1980, the Pahl murder case had more of the lurid

aspects of a *National Enquirer* story than something carried on the national pages of local newspapers. By 2006 the noses came down and the story went mainstream. The tabloids got a run for their money from everybody—the broadcast networks, the cable networks, newspapers, radio, and most of all, online Web sites where anyone could voice an opinion on the case.

At home, just a few miles away, Dave Davison, like most of Toledo's residents, was glued to his TV set. Court TV had gotten the pool contract and was in the courtroom providing a live video feed. They carried the trial live and provided highlights to everyone else. All that coverage sucked the humanity right out of the case.

Because television is a visual and not a verbal medium like radio, the heartbreaking image constantly repeated throughout the world at the beginning of the trial was that of poor Father Robinson at the defense table, old, frail, with his wispy hair and stoic countenance. He certainly was a scene stealer. This image of him was constant as the trial played out before the camera.

The staged formality of a trial plays exceptionally well on TV, especially when there's juicy testimony interrupting the more boring stuff. During the "dueling banjos" opening statements, Mandros's forensic zenith was pointing to Dr. Diane Scala-Barnett's conclusion that the tip of the priest's letter opener fit parts of the nun's jaw exactly. That, of course, implied rather strongly that Robinson had done it. The jury would then have no choice but to convict. Still, the biggest problem in front of the jury was the motive for the killing.

Why did the priest kill the nun? Mandros acknowledged this question during his opening, while making it clear that, under the law, the prosecution did not have to prove motive to prove murder. That is commonly accepted criminal law in all fifty states, and rightly so. How many times have you read about a senseless murder in your local paper and tried to figure out *why?* There is no *why?* Sometimes people kill because they enjoy it. Sometimes they do it because they get too drunk, lose control of their vehicle and kill somebody.

Is getting drunk a motive for murder? Certainly not. In fact some states allow you to use inebriation as a "diminished capacity" defense. However, it is good to give a jury motive because that is what they expect. They watch *Law & Order*; *Law & Order: Criminal Intent*; *Law and Order: SVU*; *CSI*; *CSI: New York*; *CSI: Miami*; and of course, *CSI: Dubuque* just like everyone else. In Robinson's case, Mandros alluded to problems between the priest and the nun as a "motive."

What the prosecution did not say was that they had violated the sanctity of Margaret Ann Pahl's grave in the wild-goose chase pursuit of a conviction using twenty-first-century DNA technology. Yes, they had their letter opener-into-mandible evidence, forensic supposition, not science. What they had really been going after was DNA. Find Robinson's DNA on her, and the jury had no choice but to convict.

But there was never any chance of getting Robinson's or anyone else's DNA off Margaret Ann Pahl's body. Dr. Fazekas's 1980 autopsy report stated clearly that the killer had left no hair, fibers, or blood behind. Any way the pathologist cut it, this was a circumstantial case. But somehow, the misinformation got around the Net that there was DNA to be discovered.

Alan Konop did the opening for the defense and went for the obvious—the purely circumstantial evidence in the case. The prosecution had not one piece of direct evidence tying Gerald Robinson to the crime, let alone the crime scene. He also questioned the quality of the prosecution's so-called forensic evidence. Those all added up to "reasonable doubt." The jury would then have no choice but to find Gerald Robinson "not guilty" of murder.

After a lunch break the jurors were transported to the scene of the crime, the chapel at Mercy Hospital that still exists as it was in 1980. The fourteen jurors were given a guided tour of the chapel while a bailiff read from a carefully edited document that prosecution and defense had gone over before trial. It basically identified key places in the chapel that would be referred to during subsequent sworn testimony.

In subsequent days, the prosecution carefully built a timeline of the 1980 murder using testimony from Sister Phyllis Ann, the Sisters of Mercy hospital administrator in 1980, now retired. Detective Marx, also retired, testified to how the investigation was conducted in 1980 and what the results were. Marx said on the stand that his interrogation of Robinson had been interrupted by Deputy Chief Ray Vetter, Monsignor Schmit, and an attorney (Hank Herschel). He had left the room at Vetter's orders. The investigation effectively ended there.

Terry Cousino testified quite dramatically in the well of the courtroom. With the judge allowing him off the stand and the jury out of the box, they crowded around him and he showed them one of the prosecution's crucial pieces of evidence—the much-tested 1980 punctured altar cloth. Cousino then showed the jury how the punctures in the altar cloth formed a cross. They also matched up to the priest's letter opener.

Holding the letter opener in her hand, Dr. Diane Scala-Barnett took the stand and illustrated for the jury "the lock and key mandible theory," with the tip of the letter opener being the key and the mandible the lock. It was dramatic testimony, though scientifically it was open to conjecture, since it depended upon Dr. Scala-Barnett's interpretation of evidence, not proven scientific fact. Still, it was compellingly dramatic.

At the heart of the prosecution's case was blood pattern transfer analysis. If they could convince the jury that the pattern of Robinson's letter opener was left on the altar cloth punctured over her chest, it would be another nail in the priest's coffin. Mandros had lined up not one but two of the world's five experts to testify for the prosecution.

Ms. T. Paulette Sutton holds a master of science degree from the University of Arkansas. She began studying bloodstain pattern analysis with Professor Herbert MacDonnell in 1983. Twelve years later, MacDonnell testified for the defense in the Nicole Brown Simpson/Ronald Goldman murder case. This occurred after the defendant, O. J. Simpson, tried on a pair of gloves he allegedly wore during the murders. The gloves were too small to fit his hands, or so it seemed on camera.

MacDonnell had been hired by the defense for his expertise in the science of blood spatter. At least, that's what the jury knew at the time. MacDonnell testified about bloodstains found on a pair of socks Simpson wore at the time of the murder. MacDonnell said the blood, Nicole Brown Simpson's, had seeped through from one side to the other. To him, that showed there wasn't a foot in the sock at the time it was exposed to the red stuff.

If MacDonnell was correct, that would support the defense's contention that the LAPD, or someone else— the famous "other guy" defense—had planted the blood to frame Simpson. But prosecuting attorney Marcia Clark was ready on cross.

She asked MacDonnell if it could be that as she was dying, Ms. Simpson reached out with her bloody hand and grabbed her ex's ankle. Or perhaps Simpson himself had Ms. Simpson's blood on his hands, which he transferred when he pulled the socks off.

MacDonnell told the jury that those things could have accounted for what he called "compression stains." MacDonnell concluded that in his original report commissioned by the defense, he actually described "swipes" of blood on the sock rather than compressions.

Instead of discussing gloves, MacDonnell again testified on his conclusions that bloodstains on the socks had seeped through from one side to the other. The finding, he said, indicated no foot was in the sock when blood was applied to it, supporting the defense contention that the blood was planted.

Behind the scenes, MacDonnell had conducted a gruesome experiment for the defense. He had soaked a pair of gloves in blood, in order to see how much they would shrink. The defense wanted him to testify that blood does little to shrink gloves. The idea was to refute earlier testimony in which assistant DA Christopher Darden had Simpson try on a pair of new gloves of the same style as the first set.

The new ones fit. Darden suggested the murder gloves had shrunk because they had been exposed to too much blood. MacDonnell was expected to testify that blood-soaked gloves would not shrink as much as the prosecution claimed. But the defense eventually abandoned that strategy. The judge would allow MacDonnell's experiment into evidence only if the prosecution could then introduce photos and videos of Simpson wearing dark gloves at football games he was covering for TV.

In 1998, two years after testifying in that trial and two years after the verdict, MacDonnell opened the Institute on the Physical Significance of Human Bloodstain Evidence. Ms. Sutton was the third person to be certified by the institute as a "Competent Forensic Expert in Bloodstain Pattern Interpretation."

Ms. Sutton testified that the way she figured out the blood pattern transfer of the letter opener was to first wrap it in plastic to protect it, and then immerse it in stage blood, which as much as tragedians may try, only resembles real blood. Sutton then placed the plastic-covered letter opener saturated with stage blood on a piece of cloth similar in shape, consistency, and construction to the altar cloth. In Ms. Sutton's opinion, the stains on her piece of test cloth were consistent with those on the altar cloth.

On cross examination John Thebes attacked the whole theory of blood transfer pattern analysis. He questioned it as a quantifiably reliable science, since it depended upon interpretation. Unlike DNA, it could not be given the same weight at trial by a jury. But the best was yet to come.

Even *Saturday Night Live* at its cynical best never imagined Celebrity Coroners and Celebrity CSI Types. They are a by-product of the strange intersection of commercial entertainment and realitytainment, which are now the same thing.

Celebrity Coroners are a small group of well-trained and degreed pathologists who hire themselves out to either side in a criminal trial. They are expert witnesses for a price. The publicity of being involved in high-profile trials serves to burnish their reputations in academia or police laboratories where they regularly work . . . but not all the time. For example, Celebrity Coroner Michael Baden, an excellent pathologist, has his own TV series, *Autopsy*, on HBO.

In Dr. Henry Lee's case, he was perhaps best known for his testimony in favor of the defendant in the Nicole Brown Simpson/Ronald Goldman murder case. The best part of Dr. Lee's Web site, www.drhenrylee.com, is the machine-gun fire, the constantly beating heart that goes on and on and on until you click something. It's enough to make you want to kill somebody. It's so Hollywood.

His Web site uses about a half dozen programs to present a multimedia show demonstrating Lee's areas of expertise. All the while, the good doctor himself lurks in blue shadow on the right of the screen, looking like a tough cop from a Chow Yun Fat movie. According to his Web site, the hearty Dr. Lee hails from Taiwan, where he started garnering academic honors with a degree in police science in 1960. By the time he picked up his Ph.D. in biochemistry from NYU in 1975, he already had a master of science from the same institution the previous year.

Chief emeritus of the Connecticut State Police, Dr. Lee was hired by Lucas County to analyze all the evidence in the case. He also happened to be one of the five world experts on blood transfer analysis. What a surprise, then, when he testified at trial that blood transfer patterns on the altar cloth over her chest matched the priest's letter opener. The pattern of the stab wounds on the altar cloth formed an upside-down cross.

But in the report Dr. Lee delivered to the police, he appeared to contradict this testimony. On page 10, Dr. Lee writes, "Thus the souvenir sword could not have caused the 3 inch deep penetration wounds to the victim's neck and chest because it measures greater than ½ inch in width at 3 inches from the top of the blade."

He writes in the next paragraph:

"Accordingly, appellant's souvenir sword, which is unquestionably a thick dull instrument on both sides of the blade, and which gradually increases in width as measured from the tip of the blade, could not have caused these wounds."

The only "souvenir sword" found among Robinson's possessions during the police searches was the letter opener in the shape of a sword; yet later, in his conclusions on page 23 of the same report Dr. Lee appears to contradict himself again:

> 5. Microscopic examination of the victim's clothing and later cloth indicated that the defects or holes were consistent with a sharp instrument, not a typical flat, straight bladed knife. *The unique shape of these cuts is consistent with having been created by the letter opener or a similar type of instrument.* [Author's emphasis.]

However, on the stand, the affable Dr. Lee explained that after all his tests, he could not say for certain that the letter opener was the murder weapon, just that "I cannot exclude it." On cross examination, the defense did not challenge the inconsistencies between what Dr. Lee wrote in his report and subsequent trial testimony.

Next up was the exorcist, Father Jeffrey Grob. Mandros had decided before trial not to get too involved in the ritualistic murder aspect of the case. But he couldn't very well ignore the signs at the scene either. Neither could Father Grob. On May 1 Father Grob testified that based upon his expertise, the murder of Margaret Ann Pahl was a ritual murder indeed.

He went on to tell the jury the same thing he had been telling the cops for the three years he had gone back and forth between Chi-town and Toledo. Given that the murder happened in the sacristy and on Holy Saturday, plus the arrangement of the body at the scene—obviously posed as if sexually violated, "whoever did it had an extensive knowledge of Roman Catholic ritual," the priest testified. "The blood on the forehead and the chest piercing in the shape of an inverted cross were an inherent mockery to Sister Margaret Ann and her religion."

At the defense table, Father Robinson rolled his eyes. As the trial had progressed, Robinson's image of a frail man besieged by the system was gradually replaced by a moody man who sometimes put his eyes in motion when he disagreed with a particular piece of testimony. It was the kind of image that would not ingratiate him with the jury.

But the prosecution was not looking so great either. On May 1, they were ready to close their case. They had not presented one bit of direct evidence linking Father Robinson to the murder. It was still all circumstantial evidence. That would not change, something both sides had reminded the jury at the outset.

"Call Dr. Lincoln Vail to the stand," said Mandros, who was already on his feet.

Back in 1980, Dr. Vail was a thirty-four-year-old resident at Mercy Hospital and one of the first doctors on the scene after Margaret Ann Pahl was discovered. In 2006 he was sixty years old, his intense eyes framed by wire-rimmed spectacles, with a receding hairline of silver-colored hair that made him look distinguished. Blue seemed to be his favorite color. His shirt, tie, and suit were in various shades and hues of blue.

In the twenty-six intervening years since the crime, Vail had become a much liked and respected family practitioner in the Everglades. When investigators contacted and questioned him, Vail had some new information.

He told the jury that it was around 8:15 A.M. when he heard the Swift Team call over the PA system for an emergency down in the chapel. On his way, Vail saw a priest. "He was within ten feet of me, looking over his shoulder and going in the opposite direction."

They locked eyes for a moment.

"I'll never forget the stare that just kind of went right through me. He didn't say a word and continued in the opposite direction."

"Did you recognize Father Robinson?" Mandros asked.

"I didn't know him at the time of the murder," Dr. Vail answered. "But the priest I saw was a match for Father Robinson's appearance."

"Did you tell this to the detectives in 1980?"

"Yes, I did, but they seemed interested in other things. They never asked me about it again."

Defense attorney Alan Konop was ready. He showed Dr. Vail a copy of the officers' report. Vail looked at it.

"Is your sighting included in that report?"

"No," answered Vail.

"Did the detectives in 1980 show you photographs of Father Robinson?"

"Yes."

"Did you identify him as the priest you passed in the hallway?"

"No, I didn't."

It was brilliant work. Konop had taken what at first glance seemed like an almost positive ID and turned it into a "maybe," trying to raise reasonable doubt in the jurors' minds.

When the prosecution concluded their case late on

May 1, they had called thirty-one witnesses. Besides all the cops involved in the investigation from 1980 to the present, Mandros had called his celebrity forensic experts. The question was what effect their testimony would have on the jury's final deliberations. Before that could happen, of course, the defense got its turn.

Calling the investigating officers as defense witnesses, Alan Konop tried to bring out inconsistencies in their testimony. Marx, Forrester, et al. had to stand up to Konop's aggressive examination. At first glance, it looked like they all did; none of them made a fool out of himself.

Arguably the most fascinating testimony came when the defense called former Deputy Police Chief Ray Vetter to the stand. Contradicting Marx's testimony, the now eighty-two-year-old Vetter denied interrupting the Robinson interrogation in 1980. Vetter insisted he had nothing to do with putting the kibosh on the investigation, that his being Catholic did not affect his conduct. In fact, Vetter claimed, the reason the investigation didn't continue was that the Lucas County attorney told the TPD they just didn't have the evidence to indict Father Robinson.

Next up, the defense had a forensic expert, Meghan Clement, who testified that the only DNA found under clippings of Margaret Ann Pahl's nails was not Robinson's. It was an unknown male's. The prosecution on cross pointed out that DNA can get transferred any number of ways under a person's fingernails, not only by scratching your murderer in the throes of death.

The defense had their own celebrity, and they called her now—Dr. Kathleen Reichs. Her novels and experiences are the basis for the 2005 Fox TV series *Bones*.

"Kathy Reichs is a forensic anthropologist for the Office of the Chief Medical Examiner, State of North Carolina, and for the Laboratoire des Sciences Judiciaires et de Médecine Légale for Quebec, Canada. She is one of only fifty forensic anthropologists certified by the American Board of Forensic Anthropology and is on the Board of Directors of the American Academy of Forensic Sciences. A professor of anthropology at The University of North Carolina at Charlotte, Dr. Reichs is a native of Chicago, where she received her Ph.D. at Northwestern," says her Web site, kathyreichs.com.

During her testimony Reichs candidly acknowledged that the line between entertainment and reality had been crossed. "Who's really an expert?" she testified. "Because we're very popular right now, we're really hot. We're on all the airwaves, TV, radio, and books. And a lot of people are calling themselves forensic anthropologists. By establishing board certification, we are policing ourselves."

Reichs went on to testify that in her opinion, Dr. Scala-Barnett's lock and key mandible theory had some problems. After examining photos of the tests Scala-Barnett had run, Reichs noticed the tests were conducted on dry bone, that is, all the tissue had been removed. Under John Thebes's patient questioning, Reichs explained that by stripping the bone, there is the possibility of "the potential for damage to the defect. There could be modification of the edges of the defect."

The defense rested on May 8, and the prosecution put on for rebuttal retired TPD detective Lieutenant

Bill Kina. They had really saved the best for last. Kina claimed that sometime in the early 1990s, he had been to a formal function with Vetter. The deputy chief "asked me what the nun's name was. He said he could never remember her name. He said it was 'the biggest mistake of my life,'" Kina testified.

May 10

It was time for closing arguments, and as usual, the state got to go first. Mandros chose to concentrate on motive. It was a smart decision. Besides the circumstantial nature of the case, it distinctly lacked motive, which the jury expected. Mandros addressed the issue by stating that he thought, despite the ritualistic nature of the slaying, it was done by Robinson in a fit of anger.

That was it. Anger, at life, and the way it had turned out for him. He had once had a dream of being a military chaplain. When that didn't work out, he became bitter and disappointed, dissatisfied with whatever his lot in life was.

Reviewing all the major pieces of evidence the state had presented, and the overwhelming amount of circumstances pointing to his guilt, Mandros told the jury that Father Gerald Robinson was the killer of Margaret Ann Pahl. As for the ritualistic aspect of the murder, Mandros downplayed the satanic stuff, at the same time using words like "mockery" and "humiliation" to make his point about how she was killed.

Alan Konop was supposed to deliver the defense's closing argument. As he began, it became clear that his voice was too weak to continue. John Thebes then stepped in to deliver the closing. He mocked the prosecution's forensic experts, harping on reasonable doubt, calling into question Dr. Scala-Barnett's testimony. If she wasn't a forensic anthropologist, like the defense's witness, why was she testifying at all regarding bone trauma? Blood transfer pattern analysis? In the defense's view, it was not science as much as judgment based on suppositions and interpretations.

Why was Father Robinson's DNA not found at the scene or on the victim? Because he wasn't there! Someone else had done it, the other guy.

Judge Osowik did not waste any time after the closings. He immediately charged the jury, explaining once again what the charges were that the defendant was on trial for, and what "reasonable doubt" was. He also offered lucid explanations for direct and circumstantial evidence.

Most importantly the judge made it crystal clear that Father Robinson did not have to testify on his behalf. The jury was not to read anything into that. It was the prosecution's job to prove guilt beyond reasonable doubt, not for the defendant to prove his innocence. It was almost 4 P.M., May 10, by the time the twelve-member jury was ushered into the jury room, after the two who had been alternates were let go. The jury then deliberated four hours before calling it a night. The jury got back together at about 9 A.M. the next morning to continue their deliberations at the courthouse.

At 11 A.M. on May 11, 2006, after being out for a grand total of six hours, the jury filed back into Judge

Osowik's courtroom. At the defense table, Robinson's face was an emotionless mask. Despite the diocese order that he no longer wear his collar, there it was, as it had been throughout the trial. His attorneys fidgeted like they all needed to go to the bathroom. At the prosecution table, Mandros was calmer. He figured they had either done a really good job, or a really bad one.

Judge Osowik was the calmest. Calm, cool, collected. He looked as cool and collected as a political candidate, which he was. Osowik was running for county judge on the Democratic line.

"The verdict form please," the judge requested of the bailiff.

The bailiff took it from the foreman, walked the few steps to the bench, and handed it up to the judge, who opened it and began reading.

"We the jury—"

Osowik interrupted himself.

"Would the defendant rise?"

Watching the verdict in his home on live TV, just as he had the Beatles on *Ed Sullivan* in 1964, Dave Davison heard the loud scraping that echoed off the walls of the courtroom as Robinson and his four attorneys got to their feet. There was a moment of silence and then . . .

"We the jury find the defendant *guilty* of murder."

The observers in the courtroom let out an audible gasp. Sitting in one of the front rows with the AP reporter busily jotting down notes next to her, Claudia Vercellotti blinked. She had been in the courtroom all along, every day, watching the proceedings. Even though she felt the defense had presented a weak case, she was still overwhelmed by the verdict.

"I just want Father Robinson to live through all of his appeals. If the sentence were vacated, it would be as though he was never convicted. This case represents justice by proxy, or vicarious justice for the rest of us. It's the closest thing any of us will ever have in terms of justice as our statutes have expired. It's the closest to accountability this diocese has ever faced."

Robinson was taken out a side door in handcuffs. As Vercellotti began to file out with the rest of the observers, Barbara Robinson, the priest's sister-in-law, "confronted me in open court, as her row was filing out. She stopped the entire row to say, 'I hope you rot in hell.' When I looked up, she added, 'I hope you burn in hell.'"

PART THREE

CHAPTER 13

Meet Jane Doe

June 5, 2006

It had been a long sleep. I awakened to the same gray city, only it was day, and time to meet the players in court.

Dressing quickly, having trouble as usual knotting my tie, I went downstairs to the front desk. It was the same clerk who had checked me in. I asked him directions.

"You want the county courthouse or the federal courthouse?"

"The Lucas County Courthouse."

It was about a five-block walk, he answered, giving me convoluted directions I would never remember.

"The priest's trial is over, isn't it?" the clerk asked doubtfully.

The murder trial was over all right. Robinson was sentenced to fifteen to life and was currently serving his sentence someplace in the Ohio prison system. He was also appealing his conviction. But conviction for the murder of Margaret Ann Pahl didn't exempt Robinson from other charges of rape and Satanism. What the clerk didn't know was that a new accuser had come forward.

Her name in civil court papers filed on April 20, 2005, was "Jane Doe"; her husband was identified as "John Doe." Because criminal trumps civil, her case was put on hold until the criminal case was adjudicated. With that over, Doe's had been free to go forward.

In court documents, Jane Doe claimed that Robinson raped, sodomized, and did all kinds of unspeakable acts to her during a satanic ceremony for a number of years when she was a child. She had journals and drawings documenting her abuse.

"Jane Doe had been trying to get me on the phone all weekend before she went public. My phone had been blowing up all weekend with calls from a lot the TV stations, and everyone national, and the *Blade* and everyone else after the indictment [of Robinson]," says Claudia Vercellotti. "When I finally got her message, I thought, If this is someone making things up . . . I was prepared not to be cordial at all . . ."

Vercellotti got in her Toyota and drove to Jane's house. After listening to Jane tell her story, "I didn't think the stuff was made up," Vercellotti says. "It was the old journals and drawings. I was sleep deprived because of the long weekend, but the drawings were old and tattered. This was something that had happened long ago that she was dealing with now."

Vercellotti empathized. She too had been abused by a priest. Here are Jane Doe's specific allegations from her Complaint to the Lucas County Court of Common Pleas:

"48. While Survivor Doe was vulnerable, and or in Father Robinson's care . . . Survivor Doe was kidnapped and held either against her will or through beguilement in the basement of St. Adalbert's."

Beguilement, a beautiful word to describe what in this case was an alleged act of seducing an underage child.

"49. While held in the basement Father Robinson and other clergy colleagues including Jerry Mazuchowski and their cohorts referred to each other with the first name of a woman and then their own name. For example, Jerry Mazuchowski was named or referred to himself and by his colleague as 'Carrie' and 'Carrie Jerry.' Father Robinson was named or referred to as 'Mary Jerry.' Another yet unknown and unnamed John Doe defendant was referred to or called himself 'Sue' and Survivor Doe recalls suppressed memories of him as 'the man named Sue.'

"50. The clergymen, including Defendants Robinson and Mazuchowski, dressed in nun drag, circled around Plaintiff Survivor Doe while she was on a table and chanted satanical verses and 'Son of Sam,' and their female names. They intoned that Jesus was Satan's SON. They cut Survivor Doe with a knife as a sacrifice to Satan and drew an upside down cross on her stomach. They forced Survivor Doe to drink blood of a sacrificed animal. At each instance, clergymen forced Survivor Doe to masturbate the clergymen in the circle. Furthermore, the clergymen would rape and or sodomize her, engage in sexual touching, demand and force her to suck their cock. She would try to escape, but they pulled her back into the circle and hit her. Afterwards, they would intimidate her, tell her she was Satan's child, force her to clean the blood off the floor, and threaten to kill her if she told."

In the kind of scenario Doe is describing, the defendants are classic con men. Satanism is a simple con, someone using a belief in Satan to control someone else.

"51. At other times, the same defendants and their cohorts would engage in the same or similar rituals and sexual abuse which escalated dramatically. In addition to the basement, she was placed on a table and tied down. They killed rabbits and made her drink the blood and then vaginally raped her with a dead snake that had its head cut off. They would also burn her feet and light matches, blow them out, and burn them into the corner of her eyes."

While most of Doe's account sounded like a movie, the part about the snake is strikingly similar to Sister Marlo Damon's statement to the Diocesan Review Board: "At age twelve in another initiation ritual, I was given to Satan. They used a snake and inserted it into my mouth, rectum and vagina to consecrate those orifices to Satan."

Damon's statement was not yet public at the time Doe filed her brief. There is no apparent connection between the two women, adding to their credibility.

"52. The rituals and abuse continued even after Survivor Doe left St. Adalbert's because defendants Robinson and Mazuchowski had a close relationship with Survivor Doe's mother, who also participated in the ceremonies in the woods and was becoming a high priestess."

The MO Doe alleges the defendants used was, again, very similar to the one Damon alleged Chet Warren used on her and her family.

"53. During all this time, Defendants Robinson and Mazuchowski were employed by the Diocese and Oblates as priests and teacher providing religious education and counseling for Plaintiff Survivor Doe and other Roman Catholics, Defendant Diocese assigned Robinson and Mazuchowski to swerve at other parishes and/or schools under it supervision and control of, and within its geographical confines.

"54. On information and belief, defendants Robinson and Mazuchowski abused children while serving at St. Adalbert's and his different assignment with Defendant Diocese.

"55. Defendants Diocese and Oblates knew or should have known of Defendants Robinson and Mazuchowski sexually abusive behavior yet continued to conceal their abuse and to move him from parish to parish and school to school."

The latter two paragraphs established who the alleged satanic priests worked for; time to go for the gold.

"56. Plaintiff was raised as a devout Roman Catholic and was baptized, confirmed, regularly celebrated Mass and received the sacraments through the Roman Catholic Church. As a result, Plaintiff developed great admiration, trust, reverence, and respect for, and obedience to, the Roman Catholic Church and its priests and other agents."

The word "agents" made the Church sound like it had many minions at its disposal, to do its bidding. Of course, that was the way the word was intended.

"57. Plaintiff came to know Defendant Warren as a priest and teacher; as such, Plaintiff came to admire, trust, revere and respect him as a person of great influence and persuasion as a holy man and authority figure.

"58. Defendants Robinson and Mazuchowski used his [*sic*] position of authority, trust, reverence and control as a priest to enable him to engage in illegal and harmful sexual contact with Plaintiff."

The heart of the suit was this last paragraph. The Catholic Church has, to say the least, large coffers. If anything could open them up, it would be an accusation, proved in court, that a Catholic diocese allowed "sexually abusive behavior" by a priest and or/lay teacher under its control.

To nail the point home, the brief added this:

"59. Prior to Defendants Robinson and Mazuchowski's sexual abuse of plaintiff Survivor Doe, Defendants Diocese, Oblates and St. Adalbert's had actual knowledge of Defendant Robinson and Mazuchowski's criminal propensities and behavior towards children, as well as a reasonable suspicion that he would repeat such criminal pedophile behavior in the future with other children. Nevertheless, Defendants Diocese, Oblates and St. Adalbert's failed to report Defendants Robinson and Mazuchowski's past criminal pedophile behavior and their own reasonable suspicions to Plaintiff, as required by Ohio statutory and/or common law."

This was the first time anyone had ever called Robinson a pedophile in a public document. If he had sexually abused Doe in the way she described, then he certainly could add pedophile to a résumé that included murder.

"62. Further, the conduct of Defendants Diocese, Oblates and St. Adalbert's [the guys with the money] communicated to the Plaintiff and other victim and their families that defendant Robinson's and Defendant conduct was proper. Therefore, Defendants knew or should have known that their actions would silence plaintiff and other possible victims; prevent them from discovering their injuries; prevent them from discovering Defendants' roles in conspiring to conceal Defendant Robinson and Mazuchowski's criminal sexual conduct; and ultimately exacerbate the resultant emotional distress and trauma."

Doe was alleging a wide-ranging conspiracy between the defendants, intended not just to silence her, but to silence everyone else who had been a victim of one rogue priest and one lay teacher.

"63. The sexual abuse of Plaintiff and the circumstances under which it occurred caused Plaintiff to develop confusion, various coping mechanisms and symptoms of psychological disorders, including great shame, guilt, self blame, depression, repression and dissociation. As a result, plaintiff was unable to immediately perceive or know that the conduct of defendants Robinson and Mazuchowski was wrongful or abusive, the existence or nature of her psychological and emotional injuries and their connection to the sexual abuse perpetrated upon her by said defendants."

This paragraph not only established the real damage to Doe, it reiterated her repressed memory contention to get around the statute of limitations.

"64. Defendants Diocese, Oblates, St. Adalbert's, Robinson and Mazuchowski not only fraudulently concealed and/or failed to report the criminal nature of the abuse of Plaintiff, despite a statutory and/or common law to do so, but also conspired to conceal said conduct."

Once again, the conspiracy charge surfaces, along with an added charge of fraud against the defendants.

"65. Upon information and belief, since approximately 1950 through the present, Defendants have conspired to and have engaged in conduct including intentionally, reckless, and/or negligently concealing criminal conduct of its agents, including Defendant Warren; aiding and abetting the concealment of criminal conduct." This included ". . . obstructing justice; obstructing state and/or local criminal investigation; evading civil and/or criminal prosecution and liability; perjury; destroying and/or concealing documents and records; witness intimidation; bribing and/or paying money to victims in order to keep their criminal conduct secret; violating the civil rights of children and families; engaging in mail and/or wire fraud; and committing fraud and/or fraudulently inducement of its parishioners in furtherance of its scheme to protect predatory priests and other clergy and/or agents from criminal or civil prosecution in order to maintain or increase charitable contributions and/or to avoid public scandal in the Catholic Church."

Jane Doe's attorney, Mark Davis, had thrown in everything but making the defendants responsible for John Kennedy's assassination. It was a laundry list of charges that rose to the federal level. Mail and wire fraud and violating civil rights of children and families are all federal criminal charges. And Davis wasn't pulling any punches, an interesting metaphor when you consider that he is a karate black belt and is probably the only attorney in Toledo who can break five blocks in a row with his hand.

Writing that the Church has a scheme "to protect predatory priests," furthered by "charitable contributions" was saying that the Catholic Church, specifically in Toledo, was defrauding its members by taking their contributions and using those monies to hide priests and Catholic lay teachers guilty of an extensive laundry list of local, state, and federal charges.

"66. Plaintiff Survivor Doe only recently came to know of the ongoing conspiracy and/or conduct and Defendant Robinson's involvement therein, through the news coverage of Father Robinson's arrest and/or investigation as reported on April 23, 2004. Upon seeing his picture on the evening news on April 23, 2004, Plaintiff recognized and identified Robinson as one of her abusers, and further recognized him as 'Mary-Jerry' from the basement and the woods.

"67. Furthermore, Plaintiff Survivor Doe only recently came to know of the ongoing conspiracy and/or conduct, and Defendant Mazuchowski's involvement therein, through *Toledo Blade*'s article of February 20, 2005 whereby she recognized Mazuchowski as one of the abusers and further recognized him as 'Carrie-Jerry' from the basement and the woods."

Again, by stating the memory of her abuse was repressed, Doe hoped that that her suit would be allowed to go forward despite the fact that the statute of limitations for the crimes she describes in her statement had long run out. The charge that Robinson was also a cross-dressing priest who favored nun garb was a new one, but allegations that he worshipped Satan or raped a girl had been voiced before.

The ritualistic behavior the prosecution alluded to during the priest's trial, the bizarre way Sister Margaret was stabbed, seemed to indicate that Father Robinson had allied himself with the Devil, the fallen angel of God. That jibed with Jane Doe's claims. If that could be proven in court, then Gerald Robinson would finally have been linked by direct evidence to satanic behavior.

Plus, Doe had named as a fellow satanic conspirator Jerry Mazuchowski, the church lay teacher, who had founded the nun drag group, the Sisters of Assumed Mary. It all came down to what could be proven in court. First up would be pretrial motions in Judge Ruth Ann Franks's wood-paneled courtroom.

After I'd walked for about a quarter of a mile, the Lucas County Courthouse just seemed to appear, a late nineteenth-century gray, three-story Greek Revival structure in the middle of a green oasis of a park. On the National Register of Historic Places, the courthouse has beautiful stained glass windows inside depicting the various stages of justice. Too bad someone had decided to cover the original oak and mahogany interior molding with cheap, chipping white paint.

Judge Franks's courtroom was practically empty. In the corner of the gallery, three digital video cameras were set up on old-fashioned wooden tripods. The "shooters" were two middle-aged paunchy guys and a woman wearing Sahara shorts that exposed a huge tattoo on her massive calf. The cameras all focused in the same direction, at the door leading to the judge's chambers.

They paid not the slightest attention to the legless,

broad-shouldered African-American transvestite wearing a nice cream-colored number and white veil. He sat alone in his wheelchair in the front row with his companion, the co-defendant, Gerard "Jerry" Mazuchowski. He looked like the "before makeover" on a reality TV show.

Mazuchowski was about six feet, and obese, wearing long Bermuda shorts, collarless light-colored shirt upon which dangled a huge wooden cross attached to a lanyard. Mazuchowski also wore a black boot from knee to heel on his right leg and foot. He walked with a limp and leaned on a cane. Fifty-five years old, he looked like he would be lucky if he made sixty.

Gerard "Jerry" Mazuchowski was a retired Toledo public school teacher and lay minister of the Catholic Church. He had met Father Robinson as a student, and the two became lifelong friends. Mazuchowski was a Secular Franciscan, a member of the National Fraternity of the Secular Franciscan Order. Secular Franciscans have a unique place in Catholicism. Article One of the Secular Franciscan Order states their place eloquently:

"The Franciscan family, as one among many spiritual families raised up by the Holy Spirit in the Church, unites all members of the people of God—laity, religious, and priests—who recognize that they are called to follow Christ in the footsteps of Saint Francis of Assisi. In various ways and forms but in life-giving union with each other, they intend to make present the charism of their common Seraphic Father in the life and mission of the Church."

In addition to performing at their regular jobs, many Secular Franciscans like Mazuchowski function as lay teachers within the Church. But once again, the commitment they make to the Church is much greater than a lay teacher without the Franciscan religious commitment, stated in Article VI: "They have been made living members of the Church by being buried and raised with Christ in baptism; they have been united more intimately with the Church by profession. Therefore, they should go forth as witnesses and instruments of her mission among all people, proclaiming Christ by their life and words.

"Called like Saint Francis to rebuild the Church and inspired by his example, let them devote themselves energetically to living in full communion with the pope, bishops, and priests, fostering an open and trusting dialog of apostolic effectiveness and creativity."

However, no place in Article VI is it mentioned that Secular Franciscans are supposed to dress up in nun drag and cavort through the basements of St. Adalbert's and other Toledo churches. But that's what happened when Jerry Mazuchowski organized a loosely knit group of church insiders who did exactly that in the 1970s. As the founder, Mazuchowski got the honor of naming them—the Sisters of Assumed Mary (SAM). This was prior to the Son of Sam serial killer case in New York City.

"We did nun drag. We gave each other nun's names. It was nothing but absolute fun. Camp. Foolishness," Mazuchowski later told a reporter. He claimed that Robinson had nothing to do with the group, and that SAM did not engage in any satanic activity.

Also in the courtroom was John Thebes, who ran into

the jury room, pulled out a cell phone, and started a conversation; and Mark Davis, the unassuming attorney for Jane Doe. They were summoned by the judge into her chambers. They made a strange group trudging in there, Mazuchowski, nonchalantly limping along behind them, turning for a moment to give a special look to his friend in the wheelchair.

John Callahan, the gentleman dean of Toledo attorneys, was on the phone in the judge's chambers. He had gotten stuck in traffic.

"John can you hear me?" said the judge through the doorway.

The cameras blazed away at the scintillating action.

"We're trying to come up with a date, John, in 2007 for the hearing," said the judge, "sometime in April."

"I hope I live that long," the eighty-five-year-old Callahan quipped, and everyone in the courtroom broke down in laughter.

John Callahan had volunteered his services to Robinson and was still one of his attorneys on the civil case. Callahan had told me that when he viewed the Pahl murder scene in crime scene photos, "It didn't seem any different from all the other murder scenes I've seen in my many years of practice as a defense attorney."

As for the ritualistic aspects of the murder, Callahan claimed, "I don't think it's ritualistic. What does an upside down cross look like anyway? If you look hard enough, you can find a pattern in anything."

They set a date of April 26, 2007, for pretrial settlement discussions and May 21, 2007, if they went to trial. Left unsaid was that the defendants would challenge the charges on grounds of the expiration of the statute of limitations on any charges Doe claimed except of course murder.

That was it. The attorneys and Mazuchowski filed out of the judge's office single-file, walking through the slatted rail dividing the observers' pews from the well of the court. Outside in the large corridor, in front of the impressive backdrop of the glass-walled Lucas County Clerk's Office, John Thebes cut a powerful and eloquent figure for the cameras.

"How come they're not interviewing you?" I asked Mark Davis, Jane Doe's attorney. Davis looked back at Thebes talking on camera with a hint of a smile.

"He's been on Court TV for weeks throughout the trial. They don't know me," said Davis succinctly, watching as Thebes told the cameras that his client was "not guilty."

Over at the elevator, Mazuchowski and his friend were waiting for it to arrive. Since they had no place to go at least for a few seconds, I went over and introduced myself. Mazuchowski looked at me with twinkling, questioning eyes. The elevator came and he wheeled his friend inside. The doors slowly shut on Jerry Mazuchowski's beatific countenance. He had good reason for beaming. Davis would have to get over the statute of limitations hump, which the defense was guaranteed to bring up with the court before the April 2007 hearing.

"You want to meet Jane Doe?" asked Mark Davis at my elbow.

Following Davis down the marble stairs, I paused to admire the stained glass windows overhanging the hallway. They were magnificent frescoes of the symbols of justice. Looking back, Thebes stood tall at the top of the stairs with the reporters at his feet.

Davis went out the courthouse, walked quickly through midday traffic to the other side of the street. A few more blocks, and he had gotten to his office in a warren of an old office building in downtown Toledo, about four blocks from the Mud Hens Stadium.

The only wall in his conference room that is not bare is covered with a map of the city of Toledo, with pins at appropriate points where Davis has his bases covered. During the summer of 2006 Davis was running for judge of Lucas County. If he was elected in the fall, he would have to turn Doe's case over to another attorney. He was clearly torn at the prospect.

"I think she's telling the truth. Otherwise I wouldn't be representing her," he said. "But if I'm elected, someone else would have to take the suit forward."

Admittedly, he was going to have a hard and perilous time making his case. All it would take would be for the presiding judge to say the statute of limitations expired on the charges and the civil suit would be thrown out. Davis went to a phone and made a call. He talked for a few moments and hung up.

"She'll be here in less than an hour. Here, look at this."

He handed over a huge binder, in which were copies of journal entries Doe had allegedly been keeping since she was a child. It contained extensive and bizarre drawings done in a childish hand. There were also photographs, one especially of a cute little blond girl.

Doe wrote extensively about being in a pit, buried alive. She wrote of her abuse in rhyme, like a child, with some of the entries dated 1994 when she was in therapy. The actual rhymes are written in block letters, like a child would do it. Then there were comments over some of the entries in neat script. What it looked like was a therapeutic exercise where the child writes of the abuse in rhyme and the adult comments.

About an hour later, Jane Doe and her husband, identified in court papers as "John Doe," walked into the conference room and sat down without shaking hands.

Jane Doc was a blond, built thick, not fat, about five-seven and over two hundred pounds. Her face was washed out, worn and pained. She looked like a messed-up, broken person. Her dress was plain, but her manner harsh. Her eyes twitched.

Her husband, John Doe, was no Gary Cooper. He looked more like "Mr. Goodwrench." He even had his real first name embroidered on his shirt. Bespectacled, he smiled the entire time.

During some of the early conversation, Jane Doe reiterated her charges about being abused by the two priests named in her suit. She sounded bitter and cynical.

"How much?" Doe asked suddenly.

"Excuse me?"

"For my cooperation in writing your book, for me giving you my journals and you telling my story."

It was explained that Jane Doe was looking for some sort of deal, where she would be paid to tell her story, including her journal entries and drawings, perhaps even a book deal.

"I'm a journalist. I don't pay for information."

"Then why should I let you make money off me?" Jane countered again.

Arguing the finer points of journalistic ethics was not going to make it. Jane said she had something else to go do, and she and her husband left.

Jane Doe's identification of Robinson and Mazuchowski through their media appearances was specious. Asking for money to tell her story just made her credibility worse. But the many similarities between Jane Doe's and Marlo Damon's statements were undeniable.

Dazed and confused, I walked around the block twice, trying to get my emotional bearings.

August 28, 2006

No one in Toledo believed in dressing for court except for the drug dealer who was on trial on the third floor. Not only did he dress elegantly, even Judge Osowik, the same judge who had pronounced sentence on Jerry Robinson, agreed. Osowik was presiding over the case in which the drug dealer was accused of killing a rival. The drug dealer would eventually be acquitted, to much elation in the courtroom from his supporters.

Downstairs in the second floor of the Lucas County Courthouse, I was the only one sitting in the small, six-pew courtroom of Judge Robert Christiansen, when a guy who looked like "Mr. Clean" came into court. He was a nondescript old man with a long weathered face, shaved bald head, and droopy mouth. His name was Chet Warren. A *Blade* photographer kept trying to taken Warren's picture. He held up a manila number 10 envelope that he was carrying in front of his face. He said nothing.

So this is one of the alleged devil-worshipping pedo-

philiac priests I've heard so much about, I thought. He didn't look like much. But if even any part of what Marlo Damon and others had said about Warren was true, it sounded like he was the one possessed.

The hearing I was there to attend was a minor one. Now an old man, Warren had gone to a church from which he had been barred. The diocese was seeking $5,000 in relief from Warren. It was no better than a nuisance suit, meant to assuage the Catholics who had complained that the defrocked priest was still around. I wanted to know if he touched the holy water on the way out.

Judge Christiansen ordered his clerk to bring the defendant and the diocesan lawyers into his chambers away from the public. The female photographer tried to follow the men into the back room, but was stopped by a court clerk.

"I have a right to shoot under Ohio law," the *Blade* photographer told the clerk bravely.

The clerk told her it didn't make any difference. The judge had told him what to do, and he was there to enforce what the judge said. The *Blade* shooter left with a grimace, shoving the door open, royally pissed off that she was being stopped from doing her job.

Outside the courtroom doors, Claudia Vercellotti was talking to a reporter about "my church," like it's something that belongs to her personally that has betrayed her trust. It's in her sad eyes and her obese appearance, contrasted with the photograph in her hand. It shows her as an innocent, bright-eyed, thin young girl.

"I'm double the size I was two years ago," Vercellotti

says, which she attributes to a food problem that began after her abuse by a priest.

After waiting around for two hours to talk to Warren and the diocesan attorneys, the judge instead let them slip out the back way of the courthouse without having to confront the few reporters present.

"Thanks a lot, *judge*," Vercellotti told Judge Christiansen vocally and sarcastically. The judge looked surprised that anyone would disagree with his actions.

Downstairs, the sheriff's deputies were angry that a defendant, even in a civil suit, had been let out the back.

"Everyone is supposed to go out the front, everyone," one deputy insisted.

In Toledo, even now, the Church gets special treatment.

CHAPTER 14

The Appeal

John Donahue was a Perrysburg, Ohio, attorney in private practice. Like many, the fifty-nine-year-old Donahue was riveted to his TV set by Court TV's gavel-to-gavel television coverage. Like many both in and out of Toledo, he also felt it was an unjust verdict.

"If I was sitting on that jury, I would not have convicted him based on the evidence that I saw presented in that courtroom," he told the *Toledo Blade*.

Once a Wood County assistant prosecutor, Donahue filed documents with the Ohio Sixth District Court of Appeals that he would be representing Robinson during the appeals process. A native of New York State, Donahue, the transplanted Buckeye, got Judge Arlene Singer of the appeals court to approve a motion giving him additional time to amend the notice of appeal that defense attorney John Thebes originally filed with the court.

It soon came out that Donahue, like the rest of Robinson's attorneys, was providing his legal services to the now-convicted murderer pro bono.

"That is the way it is going to be. I won't accept any public money if it was offered," he said.

His involvement in the case began when Robinson called him collect from his cell in the Warren Correctional Institution in southwest Ohio. During their conversation, the former priest asked the former prosecutor to represent him. Donahue agreed.

Donahue would review the transcript of the trial and testimony from hearings on pretrial issues, looking for appellate issues. He'd pay, in some way, for the cost to transcribe the testimony, approximately $15,000. A message to Mr. Donahue's answering machine requesting an interview was returned with his voice on my answering machine.

In no uncertain terms, Mr. Donahue made it clear that there would be no assistance to anyone trying to make money off "poor Father Robinson's" problems. In fact, the only reason he called back was "because I recognized your area code. I grew up across the river from you."

Then the message went "click," and it was dead air. Robinson was not going to talk. I knew that going in. Most murder defendants don't, especially those convicted of murder that have their case on appeal. They are too afraid of saying something to a reporter that might work against them.

As Robinson's appeal started to wind its way through the judicial system, a movement began by Toledo's Polish Catholic community not only to raise the money for Jerry Robinson's appeal, but to burnish his reputation as a good priest for the appeals court to consider in their ruling.

"This is hilarious and sad all at once," says Claudia Vercellotti. "My family's oldest friends in the world are the Mierzwiaks—Well, Dan's Mom & Joanne's mother-in-law, Irene died. So, I got saddled with making the funeral program (a task I didn't mind, it beat sending flowers that would expire in a day or so). My Mom was in the back of church passing out the programs, mind you this is an old Polish woman who died, and was being buried in an old Polish church.

"Mom says that people politely took a program and then slowly, individuals who she had already given a program to, began trickling back to her asking for another one to send to this person or that person, their Busha etc. They all remarked what a beautiful little program, and of course, periodically, my Mom (as all doting Mothers do) would offer up that 'her daughter' made it.

"Of course Mom obliged them . . . then, this little old lady comes up to my Mom and says, 'This is such a lovely program, could I please have a spare please? I want to send this to Fr. Gerald Robinson, he can get only limited mail,' whispering, 'he's in jail. This is something I think he'd like.'

"Mom said she about fell over, because she couldn't let go of the irony that my homemade program, the topic of my conversation was going to Fr. Robinson. The funniest part is I always sign my work in some fashion, but this time I didn't—it was a rush job, I was just trying to get all the pictures in it. Mom gave it to her of course, but said it was all she could do, the irony of it all.

"As I write this, it isn't nearly as funny, but it was when she told it, and it was because I can just see my Mom caught like a deer in the headlights."

Appeals attorney Donahue solicited comments from those who knew Father Robinson and wished to help him. He included them in his appeal, and thus they became public documents:

October 9, 2006

Mr. John P. Donahue

Dear Mr. Donahue,

I am writing to tell you a little about my friend Fr. Gerald Robinson. I met Fr. Robinson about 10 years ago when I was the secretary for St. Jude Parish. He is a very quiet man and keeps to himself until he gets to know you. When you get to know him you appreciate his quietness. He was always reluctant to ask for anything but very willing to offer his help.

When my mother was ill and dying of cancer, Fr. Gerry often stopped to see her when she was in the hospital even though Toledo was not his assigned hospital. He would talk with her for long periods of time and I am sure was instrumental with her peaceful acceptance of God's will. I know the talks we had were very helpful to me in reconciling all that was going on.

Even after Fr. left St. Jude we remained friends. Often times we would get together for lunch. We laughed together, cried together and tried to advise each other as we traveled life's road. Having him for a friend, trusting him is a blessing for me. I trust him with my life. Watching him in his day-to-day ministry you realize that he is a quiet man. I have never heard him utter a cross word to anyone. He always tells me to look for the good in everyone. His gentle spirit would certainly not allow him to commit the crime for which he has been convicted. He certainly is not a flight risk. For me, the old saying to know him is to love him is certainly true.

Fr. Robinson has been and will always be counted among my close friends. I do not believe he is guilty and would certainly be willing to assist if I am able.

Sincerely,

Linda M. Bugbee

In order to pay for his further defense, and especially the transcription cost, Robinson's defenders were raising an appeals fund for him, which is what the letter writer is referring to.

To Whom It May Concern:

I'm Father Robinson's Aunt. I know him all his life. Rest assured he is not a murderer. Especially a nun. He had more respect for nuns and priests. Father Bob Reinhart told me when he was vicar of priests, he told him [Robinson] to call him Bob, but [he] always called him Father Reinhart.

If you ever asked him to do anything for you, he was right there. (He always took me to the eye doctor every 3 months until he was arrested).

He never complained about his ministry in Sylvania. Even when he was called in the middle of the night and there was a foot of snow.

I don't know anyone who has the strong faith he has. He still believes some good will come out of this ordeal.

Yes, I would put my home up for him to be released.

Father told me he liked a lot of flowers for the holiday in church. The sick while at Mercy Hospi-

tal, he had John "Z" Flowers come and decorate the chapel. And Sister Margaret Pahl always allowed him to do it. If he didn't get along with her, I don't think she would have consented to his being in charge.

Sincerely,
Dorothy Siepan

Siepan's letter was not intended to, but it does fill in a lot of the blanks.

First and foremost, she's his aunt. The best thing she can say about the guy is he always shows up on time and "rest assured he is not a murderer." That's it?! Her comment about his time in the Toledo suburb of Sylvania is also revealing, showing how the diocese had hidden Robinson out in the burbs before giving him his chance to minister again at another Toledo church.

The comment about putting her home up for bail was a common one in all letters of this kind. Bail money had to come from somebody and it had been made clear to Robinson's supporters that he had no money; it would come from them. But most revealing was the comment about Robinson's tenure at Mercy Hospital and his relationship with the dead nun.

"Sister Margaret Pahl always allowed him to do it [decorate the chapel with flowers]."

Clearly, the Sister of Mercy was in charge, unless she consented to otherwise. Yet it was Robinson who should have been the one in charge. If it was hard to imagine him having an argument with anyone, let alone a nun about the way he wanted a service to go, it was equally as difficult for his supporters to imagine him killing one.

More typical is this letter to Donahue from one of Robinson's diocesan colleagues:

**THE DIOCESE
OF TOLEDO**

Secretariat
for
Pastoral
Leadership

Secretary
Mr. Michael Wasserman

Assistant Secretary
Rev. Mr. Alfredo Diaz

Adult Catholic Formation

Black Catholic Ministry

Campus Ministry

Deacon Formation

Ecumenical & Interreligious
Affairs Commission

Global Concerns

Hispanic Pastoral Ministry

Leadership Formation

Liturgical Music

Mission of Accompaniment

Pastoral Planning

Worship

Post Office Box 985
Toledo, Ohio 43697-0985

Telephone: 419-244-6711
Facsimile: 419-244-4791
www.toledodiocese-spl.org

October 15, 2006

TO WHOM IT MAY CONCERN.

FROM: Rev. Bernard J. Boff, Priest of the Diocese of Toledo,
        Director of the Mission of Accompaniment with Diocese of Hwange,
Zimbabwe, now retired from assigned pastoral ministry. Please note that my
observations are based on my past working relationships with Fr. Robinson as well
from my attendance at every session of the trial.

RE: Relationship with and testimony about Fr. Gerald Robinson

In addition to both of us being priests and serving in the Diocese of Toledo, I have
had several working relationships with Fr. Robinson. When he was pastor of St.
Anthony Parish in the central city of Toledo, I was assigned as dean of the Central
City, representing the bishop in administrative matters and facilitating good pastor-
parishioner relationships. During the five years in this position, I was never called
upon to deal with any conflicts or difficulties involving Fr. Robinson, just as you
would expect from a priest who, doing a good job, goes quietly about ministering
without fanfare or publicity.

In 1997, I was appointed Pastor of St. Jude Parish and Fr. Robinson lived in the
family home, which was in the boundaries of St. Jude Parish. He assisted with
pastoral ministry to replace me for celebrating Mass when I was on vacations or ill.
He was always warmly received by parishioners who remembered him as previously
serving as assistant pastor of St. Jude. He offered his services gratis and would never
accept a stipend .

After his indictment, I started going to lunch with him every week and I got to know
him as a prayerful, faith filled priest, quiet, with a very retiring personality. He is
definitely not an argumentative or angry priest as described by the prosecution in
their closing summary. (Claim made after final defense, did not allow for rebuttal.)

In a situation of conflict he will back off and retreat to silence. Some would see
this as a sign of weakness. On the contrary, it illustrates to me his inner strength. A
powerful example of this characteristic was given when the verdict of guilty was
read, he said nothing and showed no emotion. In an editorial the next day, the Blade
concluded that the lack of any outward sign of emotion was a sign of his guilt.
(Since when is silence or no facial expression evidence of guilt?) On the next day
during my visit to him in jail, I mentioned the interpretation of the Blade. In a quiet
monotone he responded, "In the announcement before the reading of the sentence,
the judge directed that any voice comments or noise after reading the verdict would
result in expulsion from the court room. I was merely following the directions of the
judge that no audible sound should be made."

Regarding Father Robinson's overall character, he is a dedicated , hard working
priest who rarely takes his allotted vacation time. He is a very quiet person, not
anyone who would be assertive in resolving disputes or presenting his views in any
confrontation. He is definitely committed to his priestly ministry and as a peace
loving person has not joined any causes which would involve demonstrations or any
possible situations involving conflict. Specifically applied to the testimony which
described a disagreement he had with the murdered nun, his typical response would
be to do what the sister proposed, rather than argue and continue a conflict. Anyone
with a little experience dealing with father would agree with this assessment as his
response.

Read these letters carefully and it becomes clear that no one knew Jerry Robinson. He emerges as an emotional enigma. Over and over in these letters, people claim to know Robinson, and whether they realize it or not, describe him was an emotionless, passive man.

Dave Davison decided to play his ace. The first cop on the scene of Pahl's murder in 1980, the same cop who had kept insisting to everyone he could speak to that Robinson was guilty, he took me to a diner where every waitress wore high heels, fishnet or other type stockings, a skirt barely below their waists, and low-cut T-shirts.

"Here, I've been saving this for you or someone like you," he said, and handed me a huge manuscript of more than three hundred pages.

They were all the records from his 1995 FOIA request. Even when some of those records were subsequently made public, Davison had more documentation on the Pahl murder investigation than the TPD did. The information was invaluable in setting up the timeline of the case, independent of anything the TPD said, since they could not be trusted.

"Going back over my time on the police force has forced many issues to the surface," he said. "In order to survive working for that department I had to learn to hate and I did. The people on the street were not the problem. It was the people I worked with and for. Not all of them were corrupt or incompetent but a good many were, especially in the command ranks.

"That job cost me my emotions, feelings and maybe my very soul. Over time I became like an old draft horse going through the motions of a well known route. I'll tell you what I have become. Well after I had left the department I took my McDonald's lunch to the park across the street from me. As I was beginning to eat, a car pulled up into the spot directly behind me. I heard a gunshot.

"I got out of my car and checked that car. Inside was a man who had shot himself in the head. He was obviously very dead. I yelled over to a woman who had also heard the shot and told her to call 911 and to stay away from the vehicle. Then I went back to my car and ate my lunch while waiting for the crew. I had two thoughts about all this. The man was dead and there was nothing I could do for him, and I had paid for that food."

"Get out, Dave," I said. "Get out of Toledo."

"You think I ought to?"

"Yeah, I do."

And I meant it. Even for reporters, Toledo was a difficult place. More than one reporter told me of instances when they did not toe the Lucas County line. The result was a call to the editor, and the reporter reassigned. The guys who run Toledo do not fool around.

"You know what, Dave, you won. The guy's in prison."

"I guess you're right," he said, the smile forming ever so slightly behind his droopy mustache. But after so many years of waiting for the case to be adjudicated, could he finally let it go now that it was?

I paid the check and we left. Outside, a local radio station was doing a remote in the parking lot. The DJ was flirting with a few young women.

"You know what," said Davison, starting his car up. "The owner of my favorite place to eat asked me if there would be a big turnout for me when I died. I told him the turnout would be much larger for me than any other ex-cop because of the people wanting to piss on my grave. I would have the last laugh. At least I would not be in Toledo anymore."

Davison dropped me off at the courthouse. I sought out assistant prosecuting attorney Dean Mandros in his second-floor office but got only as far as the receptionist. Mandros came out to meet with me in the outer vestibule. Anyone walking by could hear the conversation. I guess his office must have been messy. Mandros's handshake was politician-right, neither too hard nor too soft. But there was something familiar about him. It took me a few moments, and then I realized what it was.

His performance at trial had been a disorienting sideshow. Sideshows and sideshow performers are something I am very familiar with. Mandros plopped down on the aged sofa across from me and gazed on me benignly.

"I'm aware of your plight," said Dean Mandros.

I had been seeking a copy of the autopsy and police reports and been denied them. What Mandros didn't know was that the documents Davison had just given me included not just the police reports and autopsy diagram, but also a witness list prepared by the prosecution before the trial.

"The court no longer has jurisdiction," Mandros explained, because the case was on appeal. If the appeals court wanted to give me the documents, "Fine, if not, God bless you."

"What do you think of Dave Davison?" I suddenly asked. "Wasn't he the one that kept this case going?"

"We did not . . . we had nothing to do with him. He is *not* a credible person."

I looked up from my note taking.

"He's not a credible person?" I repeated.

"No, he's *not*."

"Then why was he at the top of your witness list?" I shot back.

Mandros paused to think.

"We had a hundred people on that list," he replied.

"Yes, but Davison was at the top. Why didn't you call him?"

When he said nothing more about it, I stood up to leave.

"Well, thanks for your time."

"We're finished?" Mandros asked in surprise.

"We're finished," I reaffirmed.

I needed to get the stink of the place out of my nostrils. I went over to the Dirty Bird to have some drinks and dinner. Then I called Father Jeffrey Grob, the assistant exorcist of the Chicago Archdiocese, who had testified for the prosecution.

"Is it possible the pattern of the stab wounds on her chest were not inverted but instead off to the side?" I asked, knowing that they were.

"It could have been. Like most crimes that have a length or history, with the passage of time it is open to different interpretations," Grob answered candidly. "But, if Robinson didn't do it, he certainly was involved."

"Did you say that at trial?"

"No, I didn't. What I presented I presented based on material I was given. I only came out to Toledo the day before. In all honesty, I didn't pay much attention to the trial. Locally in Chicago, there was little coverage."

But the case had blossomed into a national one and stayed that way. True crime bloggers began to question the forensic evidence in the case, in the belief, quite rightly, that the prosecution and police's claim that it was irrefutable was false. The bloggers were holding the authorities' collective feet to the fire.

Finally, I called a cab to take me back to the train station. It was 1 A.M.

In the counties south of Lucas—Holmes, Wayne, Tuscarawas, Coshocton, Knox, Ashland, Richland, and Stark counties—are the world's largest Amish/Mennonite settlements. It was therefore not surprising to see a little Amish boy asleep in his mother's lap in the station. The boy's broad-brimmed black hat was still on his head. He was not more than five years old. I thought of the boys Father Robinson and Dave Davison had been, and how they had turned out.

When the train came in at about 1:30 A.M., I walked quickly across the tracks, anxious to get on board and get out of town. The conductor directed me to a car forward. It was dark, save for the safety lights, people dozing in seats, their limbs twisted into all kinds of uncomfortable positions while looking for a comfortable one.

The train moved and I watched Toledo's gray and battered skyline fade into the distance. But sleep wouldn't come, only reasoning and questions. Did Gerald Robinson murder Margaret Ann Pahl? Was it part of a satanic ceremony?

Despite the circumstantial aspects of the case, especially the blood transfer pattern evidence, there was enough corroborative testimony from reliable witnesses, especially Dr. Lincoln Vail, to show Robinson was lying when he said he was in his room when he got the call about the murder. He was actually coming back from having committed the murder. Robinson was a volcano; he kept all his emotions inside. And he was a drinker, a lethal combination.

Robinson surprised her in the sacristy. Margaret Ann Pahl had the altar cloth with her; it was in her hands when she went down under his strangling hands. She dropped it. When he decided to stab her, he realized that if he did it without protection, he'd get his cassock full of blood. He wore, as the witnesses said at trial, a cassock the day of the murder. By placing the cloth over the chest, it protected his clothes from blood spatter. What he could not know was that it would have been minimal anyway because Pahl was close to death. That explains why none of Robinson's clothes had the slightest presence of Pahl's blood.

That Jane Doe and Marlo Damon were sexually abused seems clear. But who and how was yet to be proven in any court and probably never would be. Unlike murder, the statute of limitations on rape for both women had long run out. That meant having to go with the available evidence, which indicates to me that Robinson made the murder look deliberately like it was a satanic act to throw the police off his scent.

That blood on the forehead was a nice touch. But Robinson was so ill tutored in Satanism, he didn't even know how to properly pervert his faith and stab an inverted cross. Instead, he stabbed one that was tilted a little to the left. Then he ran, hoping not to be discovered. As for motive, it was well established that he was angry at Margaret Ann Pahl, the woman who bossed him around.

Robinson had changed the Good Friday service, which

left Margaret Ann in tears. Did they have words? Robinson will never say. But that day, he had too much and decided not only to kill Margaret Ann, but to humiliate her in death. Like most murderers, he never thought he would be caught. Perhaps he thought his god or his church would protect him.

It had nothing to do with God and everything to do with fragile human impulses that Gerald Robinson could not overcome.

CHAPTER 15

The Left Hand of God

October 8, 2006

"The hatred was palpable," said Claudia Vercellotti.

She was referring to SNAP's picketing of the "Free Father Robinson Dinner" that St. Hedwig's and St. Adalbert's sponsored at the Scott Park Banquet, a huge Toledo catering hall. Hundreds of people turned out to contribute their money in support of Jerry Robinson. It was a decidedly older crowd, as would be expected.

All day Vercellotti and the SNAP volunteers stood on the sidewalk outside the catering hall. There Vercellotti and two SNAP volunteers were in the early evening chill of an October night, holding photos of Margaret Ann Pahl aloft and questioning those entering why they were supporting a convicted murderer.

"Please remember the victims," they shouted.

When a priest was walking up the steps to go in, Vercellotti confronted the unsuspecting father.

"How can you support a murderer?" she asked simply.

People did not reply. Maybe they were too ashamed to admit that they were raising money to free a convicted murderer who was no longer part of the priesthood.

"While this is still a homicide, what makes it like nothing you've ever covered is the institution of my church and their role—this is no single 'actor' or a few bad apples—it's a bad pie. It took four and a half years of pounding here, to make this community even receptive to the idea that a priest could rape a child, let alone murder a Roman Catholic nun—we've seen a slight turn, ever so slight—since the conviction. But, not nearly enough," Claudia Vercellotti says.

October 18, 2006

Back in June, the dogged John Donahue had appealed Father Gerald Robinson's conviction and sentence to the Ohio Sixth District Court of Appeals. He did so, however, with a handicap—lack of money. It needed to be raised to pay for the transcript of the trial that Donahue had to have in order to see what specific trial issues were appealable. That meant paying the court reporter $15,000 to transcribe her notes. Robinson's supporters were trying to raise that money.

In the meanwhile, Donahue wanted to get his client out of prison. Robinson was serving his "bit," fifteen years to life, at the Hocking Correctional Facility in southeast Ohio. The attorney filed a motion with Judge Osowik to free his client on a $250,000 property bond. While the motion was not unique, the substance of it was.

"I do solemnly swear, as I shall answer to God, that I did not kill Sister Margaret Ann Pahl."

The motion included Robinson's sworn statement that he did not kill Sister Margaret Ann Pahl. Further, Donahue questioned the validity of "circumstantial evidence" that the state presented at trial through their expert forensic witnesses. The motion pointed out that the priest did not have a criminal record, and claimed that Robinson had cooperated with police in the murder investigation. The judge should therefore grant Robinson bail. His movements in freedom would be tracked with an electronic device worn on his ankle. That was Donahue's recommendation in the affidavit.

Prosecutor Julia Bates's verbal response was swift.

"He was not subject to cross-examination when he said this under oath, and it was not said in the presence of a jury," she told reporters.

Replying in a twelve-page motion, Dean Mandros wrote, "A cynic might think that this claim would have carried more weight had it been made before the jury. But then, a cynic might think that Robinson wanted to avoid being cross-examined by the state. A cynic might believe that Robinson didn't want to be forced to explain his many lies."

"It is precisely what I would have expected from Mr. Mandros. His view of the circumstantial evidence differs from mine," Donahue told the *Blade*. "He calls it overwhelming when, in fact, it is insufficient as a matter of law to support Father's conviction."

October 31, 2006

Judge Osowik denied the motion.

"The court cannot find that the jury lost its way," wrote Judge Osowik. "The defendant has not presented any argument that would warrant any suspension of the sentence imposed."

Judge Osowik said that Donahue's motion included misstatements regarding trial evidence. The appeals attorney had made two key points in the motion that the state had based its case on satanic worship allegations by an unidentified nun, and that the blade on the alleged murder weapon, the priest's letter opener, was actually dull.

"This is understandable as counsel was not one of the defendant's attorneys at trial," Osowik noted in his ruling.

"The bond motion relied on Court TV television coverage in order to try to present to the judge with my view of what the evidence was," Donahue then told the *Toledo Blade*.

As for the prosecution, "The judge outlines very succinctly the misstatements in the defendant's motion, and quite succinctly states the basis for his conviction and incarceration. We agree with it," said Julia Bates.

Election Day, November 7, 2006

Judge Thomas J. Osowik had a very good day. The Lucas County Common Pleas judge, a Democrat, was facing appointed incumbent Dennis Parish for justice of

Ohio's Sixth Circuit Court of Appeals. He won. Mark Davis, Jane Doe's attorney, was defeated at the polls in his effort to be voted a judgeship. What effect his representation of Jane Doe might have had on his election is hard to discern.

There was one other defeat that day in Toledo for a Republican running for city councilman. Dave Davison had jumped into the contest at the last minute and gotten clobbered by his Democratic opponent.

December 7, 2006

Health is not something to take for granted, especially when you are in prison. Gerald Robinson began to have medical problems and was transferred from Hocking in Nelsonville, to the Corrections Medical Center in Columbus, and from there to the Ohio State University Medical Center.

Robinson was having unspecified kidney problems that were considered non-life-threatening. Thirteen days later, he was transferred back to Hocking.

January 19, 2007

"In my opinion, Satan has won and God has lost," said Mark Davis. "I have absolutely no doubt, if given our day in court, that we would be able to prove that this cult existed and the victim was abused."

Judge Ruth Ann Franks had just thrown out Jane Doe's suit against Robinson and Mazuchowski that claimed she had been ritualistically abused by the two men. Davis, and his clients, were disappointed but not defeated.

"From their [the Does'] point of view, the abusers are getting away with it and this satanic cult continues to be protected and remains festering within our community," Davis continued, vowing to appeal.

In dismissing all sixteen counts of the civil suit, which included charges of sexual battery and violation of Ohio's civil racketeering law, Judge Franks cited the expiration of the statute of limitations for those crimes. Davis had hoped to counter that by saying that Doe had not remembered it was Robinson until the memory was triggered when she saw him on TV after his indictment.

As for Jerry Mazuchowski, he told the *Toledo Blade*, "The irony of all of this is that I would have been 15 years old when all this started. I am exhilarated to be exonerated. Dare I say, alleluia, the strife is over and the battle is won."

And Father Robinson? As usual, he wasn't talking.

Epilogue

March 2007

Sister Marlo Damon was sweating. Since she worked as an administrator in her order's executive offices, she wore "civvies," but always with a cross pinned to her front, just like Margaret Ann Pahl.

Her father had died the month before, his obituary published in the *Toledo Blade*. Needless to say, there was no mention of the satanic activities his daughter alleged he took part in. But because the obit was public, she was afraid Chet Warren would read it and show up at his funeral. He didn't, but just as she was getting over that scare, I found out who she really was.

That's why she was sweating. She was afraid I would not keep her real identity a secret. I had discovered that the *Toledo Blade* had already written about Sister Marlo

Damon, in some detail, under her real name. However, she never publicly mentioned her connection to Robinson and her charges of satanic abuse.

"I don't understand," I asked Claudia Vercellotti over the phone. "She has no problem going public as an advocate for people claiming clerical abuse, but she won't go public about her charges against another cleric that are even worse? I don't get it."

Vercellotti said that Sister Marlo wanted her identity in that context kept secret. Yet, right now in Toledo, at least three reporters on the *Blade*, all the lawyers at the trial, an unknown amount of people at the diocese and the TPD who had access to Damon's original letter, defense lawyers, prosecuting lawyers, and her own lawyers, are still keeping her identity a secret.

Why? On the surface it is the respect reporters, in particular, religiously observe for alleged rape victims not to print their names. In this case, Damon's real name has already been identified in public documents. What is fundamentally different here are her charges of Satanism, which remain unsubstantiated, and with which she does not wish to have her name associated. Nor does she want to be named as the person who got the cops to restart the Pahl murder investigation by alleging she engaged in forced sadomasochistic sex with the normally placid Jerry Robinson. That, of course, is the real point. Doesn't a man convicted of murder have the right to face his accuser in a court of law?

Mandros deliberately did not call Damon as a witness. That would have opened her to a withering cross examination, in which the defense would have intensely questioned her about her charges of satanic abuse and the lack of direct evidence to support it. That might have effectively impeached the believability of the person who, whether she likes it or not, got the ball rolling in Jerry Robinson's direction.

April 2007

The National District Attorney's Association (NDAA) had spoken. Dean Mandros had made it to the major leagues.

Nominated by Lucas County prosecutor Julia Bates, Mandros and his team of assistant prosecutors had been selected by the NDAA for induction into the prodigious Home Run Hitters Club. Each year, only a few prosecutors across the country are selected to reward work in "complicated and difficult high-profile cases."

Baseball bats and plaques recognizing their work were awarded to Mandros and his team. Dr. Henry Lee, however, did not fare nearly as well.

May 2007

Judge Larry Fidler was presiding over the Phil Spector murder trial in Los Angeles. It was in the middle of the trial that he cast doubt on the conduct of the chief defense witness, Dr. Henry Lee. Fidler heard testimony that Lee picked up what appeared to be a piece of fingernail at the crime scene, Spector's estate, where "B" movie star Lana Clarkson was blasted into oblivion.

"I find the following," Fidler said. "Dr. Lee did recover an item. It is flat, white, with rough edges. I cannot say if it is a fingernail. It has never been presented to the prosecution."

Lee denied the finding but Fidler ruled that prosecutors could present evidence to jurors that Lee had concealed the evidence. The missing piece of "whatever" was relevant because the prosecution's theory of the case was that the item Lee took from the crime scene "was a piece of fingernail with the trace of a passing bullet that would show Clarkson resisted having a gun placed in her mouth. Her right thumb was missing a piece of acrylic fingernail after her death," reported the Associated Press. That left open the possibility that in future cases, Lee's expert testimony could possibly be impeached by bringing in Judge Fidler's finding.

And Toledo? It was business as usual. With the TV cameras diligently rolling, on the one-year anniversary of Robinson's murder conviction, Vercellotti announced that she had asked the city of Toledo to remove honorary street signs designating a stretch of St. Clair Street as "Monsignor Jerome Schmit Way."

In a statement, Toledo Diocese communications director Sally Oberski said that "for over fifty years, Monsignor Jerome Schmit served our community and the people of the Diocese of Toledo with an unblemished record, developing the Catholic Youth Organization and as a founding board member of the Toledo Mud Hens . . . Responsible Toledo Police Department authorities have never claimed that Monsignor Schmit obstructed justice in the Sister Margaret Ann Pahl case, and no charges were ever brought against Monsignor Schmit."

What was left undisputed was that Monsignor Schmit

personally escorted Father Robinson out of that interrogation room long ago, avoiding a murder charge. Robinson kept walking almost into retirement and well into the millennium, where he was finally made to account on this earth for his violation of the Sixth Commandment: Thou Shalt Not Kill.

By then, Jerry Robinson had already violated the First through Fourth Commandments. During both murder investigations, he also lied to police, violating the Ninth Commandment: Thou Shalt Not Lie. That made a total of six broken commandments out of ten, a clear majority. Curiously, the Lucas County Courthouse, where Robinson was tried, has a monument of the Ten Commandments on its grounds. He went by it every day on his way into court.

As for Schmit, his street sign still stands. The city of Toledo politely declined Vercellotti's request.

Acknowledgments

Will Hinton did an absolutely brilliant job editing this book. I thank him, especially for taking out the esoteric references.

HarperCollins has been the most supportive publisher I have ever worked with. The freedom they have given me is unlike anything I have ever experienced. Their professionalism in all stages of the editorial process is like none I have ever been privileged to be a part of.

Thanks to Lori Perkins for bringing this story to my attention, and Carl Denaro, who urged me to dig into the story's satanic angle. Both Jim DeFelice and Laura James constantly challenged me to look ever more closely at the evidence.

The people of Ohio owe retired Toledo police officer Dave Davison a tremendous debt of gratitude. It was Davison's preservation of the official record of the crime scene and his insistent lobbying that kept the case alive. Without his help, not only would this book not have been written, there would have been no prosecution. Whatever someone's feeling on the verdict, there was more than enough to indict, and a grand jury should have done its job and heard the charges twenty-seven years ago.

Claudia Vercellotti opened her mind and her heart. She is a wonderful advocate for those who claim clerical abuse. Michael Price offered his expertise on Satanism. Many thanks to Mark Reiter, a splendid reporter in the great American tradition. And James Wolfe for the vetting and the line.

Appendix
Would You Make the Jury?

This is the juror questionnaire that every prospective juror in the Pahl homicide case had to fill out before being seated for the voir dire.

COURT STAFF ONLY:
JUROR #
Hearing requested yes–no
JUROR QUESTIONNAIRE
STATE OF OHIO V. GERALD ROBINSON

Please answer the following questions fully and truthfully to the best of your ability. If necessary, use the back of a page to complete your answer. Please indicate the question number. Please note that the sole purpose of this questionnaire is to help the Court and the lawyers select a fair and impartial jury.

Answer all the questions to the best of your ability. Pursuant to a Ohio Supreme Court decision: State ex ref Beacon Journal v. Bond, 98 Ohio St. 3d 146, Except for your telephone number, all information on this form may be publicly disclosed. If you believe your privacy interests will be hurt by answering any of the following questions, you may leave the response blank and, once you are in the courtroom, ask for a hearing to state your reasons for leaving the answer(s) blank.

The hearing will be held is the Judge's office, on the record, with the court reporter and counsel present. The judge may require you to answer the question(s).

1. Full Name:
2. Place of Birth:
3. Race:
4. In what community do you live?
5. Marital status? Single _ Married _ Widower _
6. How many years of education have you had?
7. Beginning with High School, please list every school you have attended, degrees you have received, if any, your major study, and the years attended:
8. Have you ever served in the military? If yes, please in-dicate the branch, years of service, rank attained, and whether you enlisted or were drafted and the nature of your discharge:
9. Are you currently employed? If so, where and how long have you been with this employer?

and please give your job title and a brief job des-cription.

10. If you are married, what is your spouse's occupation?

11. List the name and occupation of any adult children within the family.
12. What is your religion?
13. Are you a member of a church? If yes, what is the name of your church?
14. Have you developed any opinions and/or bias on the sexual molestation charges and/or convictions within religiou(s)?
15. Have you ever worked in a law enforcement or security field? If yes, please describe the dates you were employed.
16. Do you have any close friends or close relatives who have ever been employed in any aspect of law enforcement or security? If so, identify the person and relationship to you.
17. Have you or any member of your family ever been convicted of a crime? If yes, please explain.
18. Have you or any close relatives or close friends ever been the victim of a crime? If so, state who, what happened, and when?
19. Have you ever been previously called for jury duty? If so, state what Court and when.

(Please indicate whether you served as a juror or an alternate, and whether you deliberated to a verdict.)

20. Have you ever served on a Grand Jury? If so please indicate what Court and the dates of your service.
21. What newspapers do you read?
22. What magazines do you read?
23. What television programs do you like to watch?

24. What do you do in your spare time (hobbies, leisure time)?

25. Is there any reason, such as health problems, handicap, family concerns, economic or job related concerns, that might impair your ability to serve as a juror in this case? Yes No

If yes, please explain:

26. Would you characterize yourself as a leader or follower?

27. In your opinion, who is (was) the greatest American to ever live? Why?

28. In your opinion, who do you most admire? Why?

29. Do you have any concerns or strong opinions about the Roman Catholic Church or members of the Roman Catholic clergy?

PLEASE SIGN HERE:

I do solemnly swear/affirm that the answers to the foregoing questions are true and correct to the best of my knowledge and belief:

(Signature) (Date)

About the Author

FRED ROSEN is the author of many true crime books, including the classic *Lobster Boy*. *There But for the Grace of God* (July 2007), his first book for Harper-Collins, broke true crime ground with its inspirational stories of serial killer survivors.

His epic *The Historical Atlas of American Crime* (2005) covering crime in America from 1587 to the present, won *Library Journal*'s prestigious "Best Reference Source 2005" award. The award cited it as a "pioneering resource." A former columnist for the Arts and Leisure Section of the *New York Times*, he has also written frequently about popular history.

Booklist called his 2005 book *Gold! The Story of the 1848 Gold Rush and How It Shaped a Nation*,

"A fast-moving production of popular history," while *Publisher's Weekly* said of his 2004 book *Cremation in America*, "This unusual piece of writing is equal parts social history and personal memoir."

He has his own true crime blog, fredrosen.com.